# Dance
# Film
# Directory

# Dance
# Film
# Directory

*An Annotated and Evaluative Guide to Films
on Ballet and Modern Dance*

**John Mueller**
**University of Rochester**

Princeton Book Company, Publishers

Portions of this book appeared originally in *Films on Ballet and Modern Dance: Notes and a Directory* by John Mueller, published by American Dance Guild, Inc. © 1974.

Copyright © 1979 by John Mueller
Design by A H I A
Typesetting by Backes Graphics
Printed in the U.S.A. by Haddon Craftsmen

Library of Congress Catalog Card Number 78-70263
ISBN 0-916622-08-8

# Contents

# Acknowledgments

In gathering material for this book I was aided by helpful comments and suggestions from a number of people, among them:  Virginia Brooks, Selma Jeanne Cohen, Marshall Deutelbaum, Pat Egan, Richard Gollin, Madeleine Gutman, Jack Johnson, Deborah Jowitt, Ruth Lert, Judith Mueller, Selma Odom, David Parker, George Pratt, Janice Ross, Suzanne Shelton, Marcia Siegel, Allegra Fuller Snyder, Carol Teten, and Dianne Woodruff.  I am also grateful for the expert secretarial work of Janice Brown.

My work was facilitated by grants from the National Endowment for the Humanities.  Portions have appeared in different form in *Dance Magazine* and in an earlier version of this book published by American Dance Guild.

# Introduction

## The value of dance films

At a recent conference a prominent dance critic declared, "Dance has actually to be seen on a stage; you *cannot* really study it in movies." Although it certainly is important to see dance in its usually intended form—live, well performed, on a stage—a strong case can be made for the opposite point of view: dance cannot really be studied from a stage performance; to study it you need movies.

Imagine trying to study Shakespeare or Mozart entirely through live performances. No one has ever done that. Not long after the first stagings the plays were available in printed form which was surely no closer to Shakespeare's intended art than most dance films are to theirs. Music is written in a widely understood notation and can be heard and studied in piano reductions as well as, in this century, on records. Can one possibly appreciate all the riches of masterpieces like *Hamlet* or *The Marriage of Figaro* from live performances alone? And what does the student do for rarely performed works like *Troilus and Cressida* or *Idomeneo*?

But to a considerable degree that is exactly the situation of dance, and may help to explain why its analysis, history, and criticism are in such a backward state compared to the other performing arts. There are people teaching dance history in universities who have never been able to see *Petrouchka*, much less the latest George Balanchine masterpieces; there are dance critics in major cities who have never seen a work by Martha Graham or Merce Cunningham.

This inexperience derives from the fact that these critics and historians live in areas where live performances of these works are simply not available. But everyone suffers, to varying degrees, from this problem. Frederick Ashton's masterful *Enigma Variations* has not been performed on this continent since around 1970, Bronislava Nijinska's *Les Noces*, even longer. Cunningham's *Place* has not been performed anywhere in at least five years. Doris Humphrey's astonishing *With My Red Fires* has not been professionally performed more than twice in the last twenty years.

If one wants to study performances, the situation is even worse. A given dancer can only perform in one place at one time. And what of performers who have died or retired: Galina Ulanova, Martha Graham, Anna Pavlova, Paul Taylor, Tanaquil LeClercq, Igor Youskevitch, José Limón, Maria Tallchief, Leonide Massine, Alicia Markova?

Even if one lives in a city with plenty of live dance performances, one is still restricted by what happens to be available. The New York City Ballet gives long seasons of repertory in New York, but during its nine-week spring season in 1977 it danced neither *Four Temperaments* nor *Apollo*. American Ballet Theatre's eight-week season in New York had no room for Antony Tudor's *Dark Elegies*.

Finally, even if one happens to want to study a work that is being performed repeatedly in one's city, the exigencies of live performance leave a great deal to be desired. One cannot stop the performance to take notes, ask the dancers to repeat a passage eight or ten times, directly compare a portion at the beginning with one at the end, command that the performance be repeated immediately and exactly, noisily discuss the work with one's colleagues while it is being performed, schedule the performance for convenience, nor directly juxtapose the performances of the work with other ones.

Indeed, given these problems, it is rather remarkable that so much good writing on dance exists. At present, critics, historians, and other students of the dance must train themselves to get as much as they can out of the live performance, to remember it as thoroughly as possible. Unlike colleagues in the other performing arts, they must base their consideration entirely on fleeting visions and fading memories. There must be a better way.

In combination with live performances, dance films can be of enormous benefit to the study of dance. They can be stopped and started, shown repeatedly, played in slow motion, segmented for analysis, scheduled for convenience, and juxtaposed for pertinent comparison. Furthermore, if they are well done and handled carefully, films can be used to introduce audiences to the art.

Except for dance works made specifically for the film medium by such artists as Fred Astaire and Norman McLaren, it is the case, I suppose, that dance is not usually as good on film as it is on the stage. The third dimension is missing and the camera frame is too narrow (though cinemascope might sometimes be made to compensate for this latter restriction). The difficulty is greatest for works with a strong frontal orientation and large, stage-filling choruses, like George Balanchine's *Symphony in C* or Michel Fokine's *Les Sylphides*. Films are much better for solos or clustered duets, and they can be better than stage performances in works where the dancers are few in number and/or play mostly to each other (rather than to the audience) as in Roland Petit's *Jeune Homme et la Mort*, Eliot Feld's *Intermezzo*, Jerome Robbins' *Dances at a Gathering*, Balanchine's *Duo Concertant*, Humphrey's *Day on Earth*, and in many works by Graham and Tudor.

A major pitfall in filming dance has been finding film directors who are at least as sympathetic to dance as recording engineers are to music. Massine had two of his works butchered in Hollywood in 1941, and inept directors did the same to several Balanchine ballets in Germany in 1973. But, as public television's "Dance in America" series should make clear, given an intelligent, sympathetic approach, dance can be validly translated to the film medium. Even *Les Sylphides* and *Symphony in C* have been well filmed, and while the films may not be as good as a live performance of comparable quality, they are quite acceptable approximations (and of course they are infinitely better than nothing, which is the usual alternative).

The main problem is not the quality of dance films but their availability. Hundreds of films showing ballet and modern dance performances and excerpts are presently available for rental, but even these do not encompass the enormous scope of the dance art. A few choreographers are not represented on available films at all—Robbins and Kurt Jooss in particular—and others only very inadequately. No major choreographer except Astaire is represented on obtainable films in anything remotely like the way Beethoven and Brahms are on records.

What is most extraordinary, and frustrating, is the fact that while vast numbers of important dance works have been recorded on film or videotape, most of these materials cannot be had on a regular rental basis. I am not referring here to record films made to document the choreography, but rather to professionally produced films and television shows intended for, and once shown to, general audiences. For reasons having to do with unions, contracts, finances, personalities, or pure inertia, these materials lie serene and inaccessible in storage rooms all over the world.

However, things are definitely improving. New dance films are being released all the time and many of the best films have become available only in the last few years. As it is now, working only with readily acquired materials, it is possible to experience a wide range of dance compositions including works by Balanchine, Graham, Lev Ivanov, Marius Petipa, Humphrey, Taylor, Cunningham, Ashton, Tudor, Leonid Lavrovsky, Agnes de Mille, Limón, Anna Sokolow, Maurice Béjart, Herbert Ross, Alwin Nikolais, Fokine, Ruth St. Denis, Birgit Cullberg, Ted Shawn, Robert Joffrey, Gerald Arpino, Ann Halprin, Glen Tetley, Massine, Murray Louis, Mary Wigman, Harald Kreutzberg, Twyla Tharp, Kei Takei, August Bournonville, Ninette de Valois, Helen Tamiris, Alvin Ailey, Astaire, and Nijinska. Furthermore, these films preserve the performances of many of the greatest dancers of the century.

It would be exaggerating to say that the student of dance without access to a film projector is as ill-equipped as the student of music without a record player. But the analogy is gaining in pertinence every year.

# The scope of this directory

This book is principally a directory of 16mm films (and some videotapes) that feature ballet and modern dance performances and excerpts. While the concentration is on films showing ballet and modern dance, some films falling outside this area are also included. Many films that are in the "cine-dance" area are discussed and the directory also includes some materials on Hollywood musicals, with separate listings for those features which indicate choreography by Fred Astaire, Busby Berkeley, and George Balanchine. There are also sections on mime films and ethnic dance films, though there is no effort to be exhaustive in these areas.

Descriptive and evaluative notes, some of them quite extensive, are supplied for each film, and information about rental and purchase is also given. Since rental prices can vary widely (from $21 to $65 for the popular film PLISETSKAYA DANCES, from $5 to $25 for Martha Graham's A DANCER'S WORLD, from $4 to $25 for Norman McLaren's PAS DE DEUX, for example), a special effort has been made to ferret out inexpensive sources of films. Where a film's availability is uncertain, this is indicated in the notes for it. A choreographic cross-reference guide and other indexes are also included.

It is hoped that the notes, evaluations, and introductory material will be a helpful aid to those teaching dance, dance history, or dance-related courses, to those programming film series, and to those ordering dance films.

# Renting and scheduling films

To rent a film, you simply send a letter to the rental distributor indicating the film or films you want to rent, the show date (with alternative dates if possible), and the address or addresses for confirmation, shipping, and billing. Some distributors will accept telephone reservations, but they usually require a follow-up reservation by mail.

Most rental fees are for a single date but some distributors (the rental libraries of the Universities of

Illinois and Indiana, for example) will allow you to reserve the film for four or five days for the single fee. This more liberal rental policy is indicated in the list of film distributors on pp. 75-78.

A rented film will usually arrive early—often a week or more before the show date. This allows time for you to preview the film before showing it (a practice that is strongly recommended) and it can give some flexibility in scheduling. If you have any choice, it is unwise to schedule film showings for Monday, particularly Monday morning, because there is no mail delivery on Sunday and, for many people, on Saturday. Consequently, even if the film arrives at your post office on Friday afternoon, you may not get it until Monday and may find yourself worrying about it all weekend. Furthermore, Congress has recently readjusted a number of holidays (religiously observed by the post office) so that they fall on Mondays.

The film should be back in the mail to the distributor no later than the day following your show date. Late return of films can inconvenience the next renter or subject you to additional fees from the distributor. If you represent an educational institution or are renting the film from a distributor who is connected with one, the film can be mailed back at an especially low "Library Rate" which presently is 14 cents for the first pound, 5 cents for each of the next six pounds, and 4 cents for each pound after that. If the distributor requests some other mailing rate, however, you should comply.

The availability of films is seasonal. The bulk of orders come from educational institutions; the major demand is during the school year. Summer and late December showings are usually easier to arrange (you can get almost anything you want in August). It is best, of course, to order the films well in advance. Some distributors, such as the University of Illinois, will accept reservations up to eighteen months before the show date. Films can often be reserved as late as two or three weeks before your show date but the longer you wait the lower are your chances of getting the film when you want it and of getting it from the lowest priced distributor.

One can generally cancel a film rental reservation up to two or three weeks before the show date at no charge. Cancellation can be costly to the film distributor, however, because another rental request for your show date may have been previously denied. Occasional cancellations are quite reasonable but renters who cancel chronically are soon recognized by distributors and may find their later requests put on the bottom of the pile.

# Purchasing films

Most of the films in this directory are available for purchase. If you really like a film and find yourself ordering it repeatedly, you might want to consider purchasing a print. This saves you the rental costs, it guarantees a good print, and allows for repeated study or spur-of-the-moment showings.

# Sources of films

It is important to note that *this directory indexes only film distributors which rent films to the entire United States.*

Depending upon where you live, there may be better sources. First of all, you should check with your local or county public library. Very frequently it will offer films at no charge or at a very nominal fee. For example, the Los Angeles Public Library has fourteen dance films in its rental collection; Rochester (New York) has thirteen; Philadelphia has nine; Orange County (California) has eleven. In addition some states and areas have special rental libraries that provide films to residents at low fees. Among these are the following:

*Connecticut.* The Connecticut Commission on the Arts established a dance film library a few years ago and has been gradually adding to it. The films are distributed through the Center for Instructional Media and Technology at the University of Connecticut (Storrs 06268). They are available to state residents, groups, and schools for a service charge of $3.50 per film. The Commission also has compiled a convenient listing of dance films that are available at various local libraries throughout the state (Hartford, Stamford, Greenwich, Middletown, Waterbury). Information is available from June Kennedy, Connecticut Commission on the Arts, 340 Capitol Avenue, Hartford 06106; (203) 566-4770.

Films presently in the Connecticut Commission's library include: PLISETSKAYA DANCES, PAUL TAYLOR, LEARNING THROUGH MOVEMENT, LOOKING FOR ME, SERAPHIC DIALOGUE, DANCE:FOUR PIONEERS, DANCE ON FILM: 1894-1912, and the five films of Murray Louis' DANCE AS AN ART FORM series.

*Indiana.* Using federal funds (Title III), the Arts in Education Center in Indianapolis is distributing the five films in Murray Louis' DANCE AS AN ART FORM series to state residents. They will add to the film collection if enough interest is shown. The service charge is $4 per film plus return postage. Information is available from Arts in Education Center,

4200 Northwestern Avenue, Indianapolis 46208; (317) 925-9074.

*Louisiana.* The Louisiana State Arts Council has collected a group of dance films and circulates them free to all state residents, groups, and schools. Information can be obtained from Jeanne Bruno, Louisiana State Arts Council, Suite 804, International Building, 611 Gravier Street, New Orleans 70130; (504) 527-5070.

The Louisiana collection currently consists of: DANCE:FOUR PIONEERS, PLISETSKAYA DANCES, A TIME TO DANCE, AIR FOR THE G STRING, LEARNING THROUGH MOVEMENT, THE BODY AS AN INSTRUMENT, DANCERS IN SCHOOLS, and PAS DE DEUX. Money has been committed to expand this collection.

*New Jersey.* The New Jersey State Museum lends films to schools and organized community groups in the state. Users pay a service charge ($1.50 maximum) plus return postage. For information: New Jersey State Museum, Film Loan Service, West State Street, Trenton 08625; (609) 292-6313.

The New Jersey collection includes: APPALACHIAN SPRING, BRANDENBURG CONCERTO NO. 4, GAIETE PARISIENNE, A TIME TO DANCE, ROBERT JOFFREY BALLET, PAS DE DEUX, FOUR PIONEERS, A DANCER'S WORLD, BALLET WITH EDWARD VILLELLA, and LEARNING THROUGH MOVEMENT.

*New York.* The New York State Library in Albany has an extensive collection of films (dance and otherwise) that are available through one's local public library. If your local librarian looks mystified when you bring up the subject, direct information can be obtained from Auxiliary Services, Film Library, Room 1507, 99 Washington Avenue, Albany 12210. The films in the collection are free to state groups but unfortunately are *not* available for use in schools.

The dance films in the New York State Film Collection include feature-length items such as PLISETSKAYA DANCES, TALES OF HOFFMAN, MAN WHO DANCES, RED SHOES, NUTCRACKER, and BAYANIHAN, as well as shorter films such as A DANCER'S WORLD, APPALACHIAN SPRING, NIGHT JOURNEY, PAUL TAYLOR AND COMPANY, BALLET ADAGIO, PAS DE DEUX, NINE VARIATIONS ON A DANCE THEME, RUTH ST. DENIS AND TED SHAWN, DANCING PROPHET, LOOKING FOR ME, DANCE:NEW YORK CITY BALLET, IN SEARCH OF "LOVERS", ADAGIO, WATCHING BALLET, and GALINA ULANOVA.

*North Carolina.* The State Library in Raleigh has an extensive collection of films which are available

for use by state residents. Films are booked through one's local library.

Among the dance films in the State Library collection are the following: ALVIN AILEY, APPALACHIAN SPRING, BALLET ADAGIO, BALLET WITH EDWARD VILLELLA, A DANCER'S WORLD, THE DANCING PROPHET, FALL RIVER LEGEND, FUSION, GALINA ULANOVA, GREAT PERFORMANCE IN DANCE, HELEN TAMIRIS IN HER NEGRO SPIRITUALS, LAMENT, MODERN BALLET, NIGHT JOURNEY, NUTCRACKER, PAS DE DEUX, PAUL TAYLOR AND COMPANY, RUTH ST. DENIS AND TED SHAWN, and the five films of Murray Louis' DANCE AS AN ART FORM series.

*Tennessee.* The Tennessee Arts Commission has a collection of dance films that are distributed through the Tennessee State Museum Extension Services, War Memorial Building, Nashville 37219; (615) 741-2692. The films can be used by any resident, school, or group in the state at no charge except for return postage. So far, four films are available: A DANCER'S WORLD, BALLET WITH EDWARD VILLELLA, BAYADERKA, and NIGHT JOURNEY.

*Canada.* Because of customs hassles and delays, United States film distributors will not usually rent their films to addresses in Canada. Fortunately, there is a Canadian organization that has an extensive collection of dance films and rents them out at highly attractive rates. It is the Canadian Centre for Films on Art, 303 Richmond Road, Ottawa K12 6X3; (613) 922-1868.

Among the scores of films it has, or has access to, are: ACROBATS OF GOD, AIR FOR THE G STRING, ANATOMY LESSON, APPALACHIAN SPRING, BALLET ADAGIO, BALLET WITH EDWARD VILLELLA, CLASSICAL BALLET, CORTEGE OF EAGLES, DANCE:ANNA SOKOLOW'S ROOMS, DANCE:FOUR PIONEERS, DANCE:NEW YORK CITY BALLET, DANCE: ROBERT JOFFREY BALLET, A DANCER'S WORLD, THE DESPERATE HEART, ENIGMA VARIATIONS, FUSION, GALINA ULANOVA, NIGHT JOURNEY, NINE VARIATIONS ON A DANCE THEME, PAS DE DEUX, PAUL TAYLOR AND COMPANY, RHYTHMETRON, TOUR EN L'AIR, and TRIADIC BALLET.

*National rental libraries.* Although this directory indexes the dance film holdings of quite a large number of national film rental libraries, not all of them are equally important. The national distributor with the largest dance film collection and with the most active purchasing policy is the Visual Aids Service of the University of Illinois. If you are planning to rent dance films intensively, it would be helpful to have their (free) catalog with its updated supplements on hand. Also important are the media centers at Indiana University and the University of California at Berkeley, and the Dance Film Archive of the University of Rochester. Among commercial distributors, easily the most important is Audio Brandon, headquartered at Mt. Vernon, NY.

## Television, commercial, large audience showings

The emphasis in this directory is on classroom and other noncommercial showings to reasonably small audiences; the rental prices quoted are based on that assumption. Some of the films, mainly those of feature length, cost more if large audiences are anticipated or admission is charged. Most of the films are also available for television presentation or for showings in commercial theaters (many on 35mm). For information about that, consult the sales source for the film.

## Showing the films

It is amazing how people who will make great efforts to display *live* dance under the best possible theatrical conditions, will often carelessly show filmed dance under the most appalling circumstances. The film will be projected at an angle on a cracked puce wall in a stuffy room with light pouring in through inadequately shaded windows, while the sound is disgorged by a tinny speaker encased in the clattering projector. Then they complain that dance films do not work very well.

To get the most out of the films, efforts should be made to present them under sensible theatrical conditions. This holds for classroom and non-classroom showings. The room should be dark, quiet, and well-ventilated, the picture brightly projected on a screen placed so that everyone can see it without craning, and the sound faithfully projected from a quality speaker placed near the screen. If the projector can be in a booth, so much the better. Also, care should be taken to allow latecomers to enter through a door that does not flood the room with light when opened.

Marathon film showings should be avoided, I think. A typical live dance performance, after all, might consist of three twenty-five minute ballets separated by two lengthy intermissions—less than ninety minutes of dancing in the entire evening. Although intermissions need not be so frequent or so lengthy, showings of dance films should be arranged with a similar appreciation for the audience's attention and interest span, especially where the audience is a non-specialist one.

The film should be previewed before showing to make sure 1) it is the one you ordered, 2) it is thread-

ed on the reel frontward, and 3) it is not full of breaks. If the film seems defective in some way, the audience would be aided if it is warned in advance about what to expect; that is, what to compensate for in viewing.

To avoid damage to the film it is important that the projector be in good repair and clean—particularly the film gate (where the film passes behind the lens). Projectors can be quite gentle on films if they are in good condition. A series of Canadian studies found that a film passed repeatedly through any one of a number of different projectors suffered only negligible damage.

## The projector

The 16mm sound projector has been under development for a half century and the current products are remarkably hardy, dependable, and reasonably foolproof. In my experience, if handled with appropriate care, just about any available projector can do a decent job.

*Threading.* The 16mm projector looks very complicated and forbidding to many people. But anyone who can read an instruction booklet or a threading diagram can learn to make it work satisfactorily. A child can do it. Many grade schools, after all, use student projectionists.

Before showing any films, simply set aside some time to learn the mechanics of the machine. This should be done at a quiet time, not when an audience is breathing down your neck waiting for a showing. I have great faith in instruction booklets. Even if someone shows you how to operate the machine, or if you figure it out from a threading diagram, I would suggest you still read the instruction booklet carefully. There are often tips that make threading easier or improve sound-picture sync or extend film or lamp life, for example, that you should know about for best results.

*Automatic threading.* A number of projectors offer a feature that promises to reduce the terror of having to thread the machine yourself. You stick the end of the film in a slot, flip several levers and switches, and the machine threads itself.

Automatic threading is definitely a convenience but it is not really a great deal faster than manual threading, once you get the hang of it. It also can be hard on films and a few grouchy film distributors will not rent to places that admit they use self-threading projectors. Furthermore, this mechanism forces you to grind the often dirty and gummed-up film leader through your machine and makes it difficult to clear the projector should the film break or jam.

Finally, some automatic threading machines will not normally allow you to start a film in the middle of the reel. This can be a major disadvantage if you want to go over certain portions of a film repeatedly, for example, you rent an Astaire feature and, having seen the whole thing through, you want to have him do, say, "Cheek to Cheek" twenty or thirty times more. (Incidentally, whenever handling a reel of film in places other than at the head or tail, be sure not to get your fingers on the surface of the film. Handle it by the edges, the way you would a long-playing record, or wear a pair of cotton gloves, or both.)

*Lenses.* Projectors characteristically come with a standard lens, designed for classrooms, that has a focal length of two inches. If you are planning to show films in a room smaller than a normal classroom—in your living room or a recreation room, for example—you may find a lens of this size projects a picture that is too small. At fifteen feet, a two-inch lens will give a picture three feet wide. An inch-and-a-half lens or a one-inch lens would give a larger picture at the same distance and might be more suitable for your purposes.

If you ask about this when purchasing or renting the projector you may be able to get an appropriate lens at no extra charge. There are also zoom lenses that allow you to vary the picture size. This can be a convenience if you plan to use the projector in a wide variety of locations, but zoom lenses generally cost an additional $100. Also, they project a slightly less crisp picture.

*Lamps.* About the only item on the projector that will have to be replaced from time to time is the bulb. The instruction booklet will tell you how. It is more complicated than changing a light bulb in an ordinary table lamp, but not much. Projector lamps cost several dollars and are usually supposed to last twenty-five hours. Their life can be stretched if you always handle the projector carefully and never slam it around, and if, after a showing, you always allow the lamp to cool before moving the projector. You should always have a spare lamp handy.

*Speakers.* The sound is very important in showing a dance film effectively. Some projectors come with a reasonably good, detachable speaker that can be placed near the screen. In most cases, however, the speaker is encased in the projector, which means that to focus your hearing on the sound, you also have to listen to the clatter of the projector. You can get a detached speaker for these machines, but it has to be bought separately. If the film showing is in a room equipped with a good audio system, you can easily have a cord made that can pump the film sound directly from the projector into the audio system.

*Screens.* A clean, white wall works pretty well for showing films to a small audience and so does an unwrinkled sheet. But for a really bright, glowing picture, especially valuable for color films, a good screen is highly desirable. There are several kinds from which to choose, depending on how much reflectivity you need and on how widely placed your audience will be. Most start at around $20.

*Cinemascope.* A few films (particularly ALICIA and the Kirov SLEEPING BEAUTY) were shot in cinemascope or in some similar wide-screen process. This means that if you rent the film and thrust it onto your projector, the picture you see will be squeezed onto something like one-half its intended width. The film is actually viewable that way if you are sufficiently desperate, but the dancers will come out looking a bit like animated and very well-trained pogo sticks.

To correct this you need a special wide-screen lens, known as an anamorphic lens, which generally can be purchased or rented from camera stores. The lens spreads the picture out over a space seventy-five percent wider than its normal width and, depending on the projector, either replaces the lens in your projector or fits in front of it. Getting the lens to work exactly without any distortion or focus problems can be a bit tricky and you should practice a bit with it before using it for an audience.

*Still frame.* Many 16mm projectors allow one to stop in mid-film, holding a single frame on the screen. This feature can be extremely helpful for taking down credits on a film and it also has some limited value in analyzing a dance—though the art form, of course, is considerably more than a series of stills.

*Slow motion.* There are analyst projectors, popular with football coaches, that allow one to vary the speed of the film at will, and to back it up freely. They tend to be quite expensive, however, and mostly slow the film down to very low speeds—fifty percent and less.

Most standard classroom projectors come equipped with a kind of slow motion that can often be helpful in analyzing dance patterns. They are able to project the film at "silent speed," which runs the projector at 18 frames per second, as well as at the usual "sound speed" standard of 24 frames per second. "Silent speed" is often an excellent pace at which to look at dance; the choreography is slowed down, but not so much that it loses its continuity. Furthermore, the sound can remain on although its quality will be less good and the pitch will drop, but the music will still be listenable.

Some old films, particularly portions of Pavlova's dancing on IMMORTAL SWAN and on BALLET FOR ALL—5, were originally shot at a slower speed and, to avoid having the dancer seem to frolic around at a goofy Chaplinesque pace, the films should be projected at "silent speed" (with the sound left on).

*Cost of rental and purchase.* Rentals of 16mm sound projectors can readily be arranged through camera and photographic stores. A typical rental is $20-$25 for a day or weekend. Public libraries are also a good source.

It costs at least $600 to buy a new projector. This is a pretty hefty sum, of course, but it should be kept in mind that the machines are likely to give many years of reliable service. Shop around for discounts, either as an individual or through a group or school—and see below.

# A source of inexpensive projectors and other equipment

Tucked away rather improbably in the Catskill Mountains is a warehouse packed with 16mm projectors and accessory equipment. It is the domain of Harold Hecht, who buys the equipment used, often in large lots, repairs and reconditions the items that need it, and then sells at bargain prices.

Hecht has classroom-type projectors on sale for as low as $140, scarcely any going for more than $400. He also sells powerful models designed for large auditoriums at comparable price reductions, as well as: projection lenses; accessory speakers; voltage control devices; slide, filmstrip, opaque, and overhead projectors; splicers; and rewinds. In addition, he has some cameras, copiers, lighting equipment, tape recorders, and 8mm projectors.

Everything Hecht sells comes with a ten-day guarantee—if you don't like what you get, send it back and he will refund your money. Furthermore, there is a thirty-day warranty on parts and labor. In either case you only have to pay the shipping costs.

As it happens, the 16mm projector is a rather hardy beast. If properly cared for it can give decades of excellent service. There are plenty of World-War-II-vintage projectors around still performing beautifully. Consequently, used models are not necessarily inferior to new ones. In fact, recent improvements in 16mm projectors—to make them lighter or self-threading or transistorized—often make them more complicated, less hardy, and far costlier to repair than the old monsters. For example, Hecht himself recommends the older model Bell and Howell machine

rather than the more expensive current models (which he also handles). He finds the old models were manufactured to superior standards and specifications.

The kind of projector you need will depend on the uses you plan for it. Different models would be recommended, for example, if you'll have to lug the thing around a lot rather than letting it sit in one location all the time. Or if you need to use it in a large room rather than in a small apartment. Or if you have a single use in mind rather than a large variety of uses. Or if you think you would have a need for slow motion or still frame features or not. Hecht has a reputation for being helpful in answering queries about individual requirements and for making honest recommendations. The Hecht Film and Equipment Corporation can be reached at Box 443, Ellenville, NY 12428. The phone is (914) 647-6334.

Another source of reconditioned 16mm projectors, sold with a warranty, is Titanic, P.O. Box 6357, Cincinnati, OH 45206.

# Putting on a dance film series

Assembling and then showing a series of dance films often seems an attractive and inexpensive way to expand dance interest in one's community or school. Such an enterprise should be planned with care, however. It is vitally important that the films be screened under sensible theatrical conditions (see the section on "Showing the films" above), and it is wise to hold each film session to a reasonable length—say seventy-five to ninety minutes.

It is often helpful to the audience to have a program with each film session. It could furnish cast lists, information about the work and the dancers to be seen, some historical background, and so forth. A brief verbal introduction is also frequently enlightening. Information or commentary from this directory may be of some aid in this.

Below is a list of films that might be considered in planning a dance film series. Suggested are a number of ballet, modern dance, and cine-dance 16mm films that, I think, would be enjoyable and attractive both to general and to dance-oriented audiences. It could provide a basis from which to select films. For each film, a capsule description is given together with the running time and the price charged by the most economical rental source (a few may cost more if you charge admission). Further information, of course, can be found under the film's listing in this directory.

The following list stresses films that tend to appeal to a variety of audiences, that rent for no more than

$150, and that are readily available. There are many other good dance films, some of which may suit your specific audience better, particularly if it has a special interest. So while these suggestions may serve as a rough introductory guide, it would be wise in addition to look through the directory for other possibilities to suit your special needs.

| Lowest rental ($) | Minutes (c=color) | Title, brief description |
|---|---|---|
| 5 | 7 | AIR FOR THE G STRING (Humphrey lyric work) |
| 24 | 54c | ALVIN AILEY—MEMORIES AND VISIONS (excerpts) |
| 150 | 90c | AMERICAN BALLET THEATRE (*Pillar of Fire* and excerpts) |
| free | 25c | ANATOMY LESSON (Tetley work) |
| 6 | 10c | BALLET ADAGIO (slow motion duet) |
| 12 | 27c | BALLET WITH EDWARD VILLELLA (demonstration, excerpts) |
| 6 | 29 | DANCE: NEW YORK CITY BALLET (Balanchine duets) |
| 6 | 30 | DANCER'S WORLD (Graham talk and demonstration) |
| 50 | 85c | EVENING WITH ROYAL BALLET (Fonteyn/Nureyev) |
| free | 15c | FUSION (Nikolais cine-dance) |
| 11 | 37 | GALINA ULANOVA (documentary, excerpts) |
| 9 | 11c | IN A REHEARSAL ROOM (romantic duet) |
| 22 | 54c | MARGOT FONTEYN (documentary, excerpts) |
| 8 | 4 | OLYMPIA DIVING SEQUENCE (cine-dance) |
| 4 | 14 | PAS DE DEUX (McLaren multiple images) |
| 12 | 33c | PAUL TAYLOR AND CO. (documentary, excerpts) |
| 22 | 70 | PLISETSKAYA DANCES (documentary, excerpts) |
| 75 | 126c | ROMEO AND JULIET BALLET (Fonteyn/Nureyev) |
| 75 | 92c | SLEEPING BEAUTY (Kirov) *Cinemascope* |
| 21 | 59c | SUE'S LEG/REMEMBERING THE 30s (Tharp) |
| 45 | 101 | TOP HAT (Astaire/Rogers) |
| 21 | 50c | TOUR EN L'AIR (show with BALLET ADAGIO) |
| 9 | 15c | YOUNG MAN AND DEATH (Petit work with Nureyev) |

*The following films are also recommended, but should probably be given second consideration.*

| Lowest rental ($) | Minutes (c=color) | Title, brief description |
|---|---|---|
| 10 | 22c | ACROBATS OF GOD (Graham comic work) |
| 12 | 14 | ADAGIO (atmospheric) |
| 7 | 22 | ADOLESCENCE (on training) |
| 13 | 40 | ANNA SOKOLOW DIRECTS—ODES (rehearsals and performance) |
| 60 | 81 | BALLERINA (Verdy) |
| 14 | 29 | BALLET FOR ALL—7 (Ashton's *Fille*) |
| 8 | 29 | DANCE—A REFLECTION (Ross' *Caprichos*) |
| 6 | 29 | DANCE: ROBERT JOFFREY BALLET (excerpts) |
| 4 | 9 | DESPERATE HEART (Bettis) |
| 11 | 12 | EARLY DANCE FILMS (goofy excerpts) |
| 27 | 33c | ENIGMA VARIATIONS (Ashton's work) |
| 8 | 12 | ETERNAL CIRCLE (Kreutzberg) |
| 9 | 20c | GAY PARISIAN (Massine) |
| 7 | 27 | GRADUATION BALL (Lichine) |
| 30 | 36 | IMMORTAL SWAN (Pavlova excerpts) |
| 8 | 5c | INCENSE (St. Denis) |
| 16 | 22c | LIGHT, PART 5 (avant-garde) |
| 55 | 85c | LITTLE HUMPBACKED HORSE (Plisetskaya) |
| 27 | 89c | MARTHA GRAHAM DANCE CO. (several works) |
| 50 | 28c | MOTION (Murray Louis) |
| 6 | 13 | NINE VARIATIONS ON A DANCE THEME (cine-dance) |
| 10 | 23 | PAKHITA (Petipa divertissement) |
| 65 | 133c | RED SHOES (classic feature) |
| 4 | 10 | RUSSIAN BALLET AND FOLK DANCES |
| 7 | 30 | RUTH ST. DENIS AND TED SHAWN (talk, dance) |
| 13 | 27 | SCENES FROM THE BALLET OF FOUNTAIN OF BAKHCHISARAI (Soviet ballet) |
| 25 | 43 | SCHOOL OF AMERICAN BALLET (documentary) |
| 6 | 10 | SPRING NIGHT (Lichine/Gollner) |
| 13 | 52 | SWEDEN: FIRE AND ICE (Cullberg's *Miss Julie*) |
| 19 | 30c | WITH MY RED FIRES (Humphrey drama) |
| 65 | 70 | WORLD'S YOUNG BALLET (Moscow competition) |

# The use of dance films, particularly in the college classroom

Since students in courses on the novel spend much time reading novels and students in music courses listen to a great deal of music, the students in a comparable course on dance should be seeing a generous quantity of dance. One can lecture about dance history and aesthetics, show slides and play records, or arrange for demonstrations of dance technique. But, in my view, the students should principally experience dance compositions in finished form, as complete works of art.

Live performances would be best for this, of course. But in most places they can hardly be relied upon. Performances by professional groups passing through town can be structured into the course, but the widest variety of dance can be absorbed through a selective showing of dance films. As noted earlier, the film medium offers certain advantages: performances can be scheduled to the demands of the course, a wide range of dance compositions and performances can be viewed, and the compositions can be replayed and segmented for analysis.

In handling the films, considerable preparation is generally necessary, sometimes amounting to a full rehearsal. Each film should be previewed before the class session and a presentation organized. A verbal introduction, sometimes with slides or mimeographed program notes might be given for each film. In this, efforts can be made to place the dance composition in historical context, to discuss the choreographer's approach, to supply musical or literary references, to introduce the dancers, and to warn about any film defects.

It is frequently helpful to comment as the film progresses, suggesting things to watch for, pointing out dance ideas or elements of structure that seem especially significant. This procedure often helps to engage and retain the students' interest. A lot of specific material presented before the showing tends to be forgotten by the time the relevant portion of the film is screened (often leading to strained efforts to read notes in the dark).

Then, part of the film—or all of it, if short—can be reshown, sometimes with stop action or slow motion (very hard to arrange in live performance). This allows closer and more detailed analysis. In general, the films need not be treated as if they were sacrosanct. They often have been created for different purposes and one should feel free to use them in a manner that best serves the educational or theatrical purpose at hand. This may mean screening only parts of some films, while dwelling intensely on other films and showing them repeatedly.

Sometimes even bad films can be used profitably if they are handled carefully. And, under certain circumstances, productive use can be made of record films—films in which a single, immobile camera has been set up at the back of the theater and is simply turned on while the dance composition is performed on the stage. The NEW DANCE film is an example. Such a film will have a band of activity across the central portion, while the bottom (orchestra pit) and top will generally be black. (One way to handle such films is to show them twice as large as usual, using a projector lens with a short focal length such as one inch instead of two. The band of dance activity can be spread across two screens set side-by-side or across a wide wall while the top black is "projected" on the ceiling and the bottom black on the floor.) Faces tend to be indistinct on record films but the spatial integrity of the choreography, so often sabotaged by mindless camera and editing gimmickry and pointless closeups in other films, will be preserved. Success will depend, of course, on a good performance, and it is usually best if the dance is costumed and well lit, filmed with sound and in color.

Once again it should be stressed that it is absolutely essential to present the films under the best possible physical conditions of projection, sound reproduction, sight lines, and room ventilation; in other words, under sensible theatrical conditions. It takes a special degree of attentiveness and involvement to get the most out of the films, so one should minimize the obstacles for the students. For the same reason, short class sessions, probably no longer than seventy-five minutes, seem a good idea. Marathon film showings are likely to be counterproductive.

Rental fees for a course making extensive use of films can start at $350 and could run much higher. As noted above, local public libraries usually have a few dance films available at low rentals and sometimes nearby dance schools and universities or their dance departments have film collections. Some expensive films probably have broad appeal and university film societies might be enticed to show them, meeting rents out of admission fees. Since rental prices may vary considerably from distributor to distributor, care in ordering films can substantially reduce costs. In addition, those who order well in advance are more likely to be able to get them from the least expensive sources.

# Available films: an overview

While every dance composition one might want to show to a class or to an audience may not be available on film, a wide variety is available. The following discussion attempts to give some guidelines and suggestions about quality and availability. It presents in rough chronological order choreographers and choreographic periods as they are available on film, with suggestions on how the films might be presented. The suggestions, of course, simply reflect personal experience and tastes and would need substantial modification or outright abandonment by someone with different perspectives or a different approach. The discussion should be read in that light.

Although choreographers and choreographic periods are stressed in the discussion, it also happens that the films preserve the performances of many of the greatest dancers of the last forty years. And it should also be noted that there is some preoccupation with duets and solos, which of course are relatively easy to photograph. Further notes and rental and sales information for each film appear in the directory.

Items in capital letters are film titles.

*Ballet before Bournonville.* Although there has been quite a bit of careful work on reconstructing dance and dance styles of the pre-Romantic ballet, little of this has yet found its way onto available film. Some limited examples can be seen on BALLET FOR ALL—1.

*Bournonville.* The only examples are danced by non-Danish dancers: BALLET FOR ALL—1 has about six minutes from *Konservatoriet* (1849) and BALLET FOR ALL—2 has the sylph's opening dance from Bournonville's *La Sylphide* (1836). (Danish television once did an elaborate series of programs on the Bournonville technique. The programs are locked up in Copenhagen under such tight restrictions that they may not be shown for educational purposes even in Denmark.)

*Giselle.* There is a fine film of the complete 1841 ballet with Alicia Alonso: GISELLE. Ulanova's largely complete version on BOLSHOI BALLET is available only on 35mm at present.

A pretty good introduction to the ballet is the scaled-down set of excerpts on BALLET FOR ALL—2. One could also show GALINA ULANOVA, a fine documentary on the great ballerina which includes nearly ten minutes from Act I: the wooing and the mad scenes.

The Kaye/Youskevitch GISELLE has its virtues, but it is of such poor visual quality and the dancers were under such severe spatial restrictions that it is really basically a curiosity item for specialist audiences.

*Coppélia.* A substantial consideration of this 1870 ballet and of the various ways it has been performed is included on the film BALLET FOR ALL—3.

*Petipa.* There is quite a bit of Petipa on various films. Very impressive is a SLEEPING BEAUTY (1890) virtually complete (no *Bluebird* variations or coda, unfortunately), danced by the Kirov Ballet led by Alla Sizova and the late Yuri Solovyov (in cinemascope only, see p. 60. If the sound is loud (but not distorted, of course), the Tchaikovsky score can be a big help in putting this ballet across—as it does in the theater.

The last act of this ballet (called *Aurora's Wedding* when performed separately) is available in more complete form on the splendid EVENING WITH THE ROYAL BALLET—PART 2. (The reel also includes Margot Fonteyn and Rudolf Nureyev in a spectacular *Corsaire Pas de Deux*.) Fonteyn's warm, sensitive Aurora can be compared to Sizova's cooler, more athletic performance. Fonteyn's superb performance of the "Rose Adagio" from Act I of the ballet is on the film MARGOT FONTEYN.

Other comparisons are also possible. Doreen Wells and David Wall dance the adagio from the *Sleeping Beauty Pas de Deux* on BALLET FOR ALL—4 and the adagio and female variation are found among the numerous Petipa excerpts on the popular PLISETSKAYA DANCES. Also on this latter film are some explosive excerpts from *Don Quixote* which can, in part, be compared to a performance by Olga Lepeshinskaya of *Don Quixote* solo variations on RUSSIAN BALLET AND FOLK DANCES or on BALLET CONCERT. Plisetskaya is fiery and sexy while Lepeshinskaya is impish and lovable.

Excellent examples of Petipa at his wittiest are displayed on the inexpensive PAQUITA (PAKHITA). Complete performances of versions of the *Black Swan Pas de Deux* are on two expensive films: AMERICAN BALLET THEATRE: A CLOSE-UP IN TIME and ALICIA. See also DON QUIXOTE.

*Ivanov.* An intelligent discussion of the famous adagio from Act II of *Swan Lake* (1895) is found on BALLET FOR ALL—4 (danced by Wells and Wall). A Tallchief/Eglevsky performance of the adagio is on CLASSICAL BALLET and Ulanova's somewhat shortened version is found on several films including the *Swan Lake* on STARS OF THE RUSSIAN BALLET. The twenty-three minute, outdoor SWAN LAKE should be avoided at all costs. Best of all is a sixteen-minute passage from Act II on the fine color film, ROYAL BALLET, with Fonteyn and Michael Somes. It has a corps de ballet, incorporates the Prince's friend, Benno, into the adagio as in the original version, and also includes the waltz, the cygnet quartet, the "rondo," and the basic action of the act.

Some Ivanov survives on THE NUTCRACKER film, but the production is garishly overdressed and overdecorated and, at least on some prints, the sound is partly out of sync.

*Fokine.* A fine, complete *Les Sylphides* (1909), in color, with Fonteyn and Nureyev is included on EVENING WITH THE ROYAL BALLET—PART 1. Fonteyn fans may want to compare the 1947 clips, MARGOT FONTEYN IN "LES SYLPHIDES," but this film has little value on its own.

Portions of *Petrouchka* (1911) are fairly well danced on BALLET FOR ALL—5. The ballet should be more fully explained, however, and viewers filled in on the missing scenes.

(There are some fine passages from the second scene of *Petrouchka*, with Michael Smuin, on FIRST POSITION, but the availability of this film is uncertain.) A warmly humorous and very attractive *Firebird* (1910) is on ROYAL BALLET, danced by Fonteyn and Somes.

*Nijinsky.* Vaslav Nijinsky apparently was never filmed, but one can convey some appreciation for his stage presence by showing slides of him in various roles. A film has been made of his 1912 work, AFTERNOON OF A FAUN, using some sixty stills and contemporary drawings in coordination with the Debussy score. Portions of the Ballet Rambert version of this ballet (which seems to match the Nijinsky photographs only very approximately) can be found on BALLET FOR ALL—6 and can be compared to the other film.

*Late Diaghilev.* Only three dance passages from this period are available on film at present. One of these is a two-and-a-half-minute solo from Balanchine's *Apollo* (1928) on BALLET WITH EDWARD VILLELLA. The performance is superb and should certainly be shown more than once. Slides and discussion can be used to set the solo in context.

Included on BALLET FOR ALL—6 are two other excerpts: the hostess' solo from Nijinska's *Les Biches* (1924), beautifully performed by Deanne Bergsma, and the cancan duet from Massine's *Boutique Fantasque* (1919). A duet from Massine's *Beau Danube*—choreographed in 1924 for a different company—appears on GREAT PERFORMANCE IN DANCE.

The René Clair film, ENTR'ACTE (1924), might be used to illustrate some of the zany experimentation that was characteristic of Diaghilev's Paris of the 1920s.

*Schlemmer.* Artistic experimentation in the Germany of the 1920s can be illustrated with two films:

an interesting reconstruction of Oskar Schlemmer's famous 1922 work, TRIADISCHE BALLETT, and a documentary demonstration of his approach on MENSCH UND KUNSTFIGUR. Both films are free but are sometimes difficult to schedule.

*Pavlova.* Anna Pavlova was filmed several times in the 1920s. Music was later added to some of these silent films and a selection appears on THE IMMORTAL SWAN, while Pavlova's version of Fokine's *Dying Swan* can be found on BALLET FOR ALL—5. Suggestions about the proper projection speeds for these films are included in the directory.

Plisetskaya's famous and very different version of *Dying Swan* is on PLISETSKAYA DANCES and Ulanova's is on BALLET CONCERT. If handled carefully, the film effort to reconstruct Fokine's original intention, DYING SWAN, can be instructive in comparison with these films.

*Modern dance before the 1930s including Ruth St. Denis and Ted Shawn.* Slides must presently suffice for Isadora Duncan and Loie Fuller, though at least one film of the latter does exist. On the other hand there is quite a bit of material on Ruth St. Denis. The best single record is a 1953 color film of her INCENSE (1906). It is obtainable either by itself or connected to four other numbers on RUTH ST. DENIS BY BARIBAULT. Also valuable is RUTH ST. DENIS AND TED SHAWN. Walter Terry's chatty commentary is informative and the interview material by Shawn and St. Denis seems suggestive of their personalities and relationship. The only Shawn dance available (there is a fine silent *Kinetic Molpai* from the 1930s somewhere) is the *Japanese Warrior* solo that appears on this film. DENISHAWN shows charming newsreel footage of the school in 1915 and some brief, frisky St. Denis solos filmed with sound about 1930. RADHA is mostly for specialized interests; the appalling film DANCING PROPHET should be avoided.

Some strange, curious, and generally wonderful examples of turn-of-the-century skirt and variety dancing are on EARLY DANCE FILMS. The film, INTRODUCTION TO DUNCAN DANCES seems to represent some of Duncan's choreography, but the performances are poor. See also DANCE ON FILM.

The effect on other choreographers of St. Denis' stylized and carefully planned use of wraps and veils, as demonstrated particularly in the *White Jade* solo on the Baribault film, is apparent in two works from the 1920s: Graham's FLUTE OF KRISHNA and a beautiful film of Humphrey's AIR FOR THE G STRING. Both works, of course, also have other points of interest.

*Wigman and Kreutzberg.* Mary Wigman is seen performing four solos, including portions of the legendary *Witch Dance,* on the extraordinary 1929 sound film MARY WIGMAN: FOUR SOLOS. This may be the only time she was filmed dancing.

A Harald Kreutzberg solo work from the 1930s was brilliantly transferred onto film in 1952: THE ETERNAL CIRCLE. Also of interest is Kreutzberg's impressive appearance as a disease-bearing jester in the 1943 German feature, PARACELSUS.

*Tamiris.* The choreographer performs to great effect five of her solos, choreographed around 1930, on HELEN TAMIRIS IN HER NEGRO SPIRITUALS.

*Ballet in the 1930s: Massine, Lichine, and de Valois.* None of Massine's symphonic ballets from the 1930s is available on film, but two of his lighter works are: GAY PARISIAN (GAIETE PARISIENNE) and SPANISH FIESTA (CAPRICCIO ESPAGNOL). The former is the better of the two. Massine appears with the Ballet Russe de Monte Carlo in both films, demonstrating a kind of character dancing that is difficult to see on the stage nowadays. (Further demonstration by Massine, along with Robert Helpmann and Frederick Ashton, can be found on TALES OF HOFFMANN.) The two films are overdirected, with almost as many camera angles as dance steps, and the plot, such as it is, becomes obscured, particularly in GAY PARISIAN. Commentary during the film showing can be helpful, at least to clarify which of the twirling, bubbling, flirtatious damsels is, after all, the Glove Seller.

Another film that shows the same kind of ballet is David Lichine's 1940 work, GRADUATION BALL. Also of interest: Lichine's 1935 film, SPRING NIGHT.

Excerpts from de Valois' 1935 ballet *The Rake's Progress,* very well performed, are on BALLET FOR ALL—6.

*Humphrey.* Humphrey's *Passacaglia* (1938) is presented on DANCE: FOUR PIONEERS, a fine film that also includes documentary material on the values and personalities of the Bennington modern dance movement of the 1930s. To show what the pioneer modern dancers were rebelling against, GAIETE PARISIENNE or GRADUATION BALL can be used. Extended notes for the Humphrey film are available as an aid.

Humphrey's dramatic side is brilliantly exemplified in her remarkable 1936 work, WITH MY RED FIRES and in the exquisite DAY ON EARTH (choreographed in 1947). For specialized study the record (fixed camera) version of *With My Red Fires* is helpful. Also valuable are NEW DANCE and VARIATIONS AND CONCLUSION OF NEW DANCE from the mid-1930s, though these are available only in a record (fixed camera) version and should be used with care.

Two versions of Humphrey's 1931 work, SHAKERS, can be obtained, and they make an interesting contrast. One is an Ohio State University student performance, with sound and on a stage, that can be compared to Thomas Bouchard's silent film interpretation from 1940 set in a studio that suggests a Shaker meeting house. Bouchard's film is rather over-rich in camera and editing gimmicks, but it features as dancers Doris Humphrey, Charles Weidman, and José Limón. It becomes clear that, while the students have done quite a good job, they do not approach the intensity generated by the earlier cast. For example, at the end the Shaker ritualists are required to leap spread-eagle into the air several times until, satiated, they fall to their knees assuming a gesture of pious serenity. The students perform this expression of religious catharsis competently, but the earlier cast delivers it with a terrifying frenzy.

Also notable is Humphrey's 1928 work, AIR FOR THE G STRING. Humphrey dances on this beautiful sound film.

*Weidman.* A reasonably good film of his 1941 spoof, FLICKERS, is available.

*Graham.* What many people take to be quintessential Graham is on display in the excellent film of her examination of the Oedipus myth, NIGHT JOURNEY, choreographed in 1947. It is a film that should be prefaced with an introduction (extended notes for it are available).

This is also true of CORTEGE OF EAGLES, a work from 1967. The flurry of characters in a story that is unfamiliar to many can cause utter bewilderment: who are all those people to Hecuba and Hecuba to them? The dramatic construction of this powerful work is outlined in the notes to its listing in the directory, and may be helpful as a guide.

On the other hand, the superb film, A DANCER'S WORLD (1957), and the film of her comic 1960 work, ACROBATS OF GOD, require little embellishment. In A DANCER'S WORLD, after completing her discussion of the dancer's art and craft and after her company has demonstrated her dance vocabulary, Graham sweeps onto the stage to perform the role of Jocasta in NIGHT JOURNEY; some like to program the two films together for that reason.

APPALACHIAN SPRING and SERAPHIC DIALOGUE, works from 1944 and 1955 respectively, may need some minor clarification about the characters—one should probably be prepared in Seraphic Dialogue for four manifestations of Joan of Arc, for example—and some commentary about Graham's approach.

A 1976 film, MARTHA GRAHAM DANCE COMPANY, from the "Dance in America" series greatly expands the opportunity to study this great choreographer. Included on this film are fine performances of the lyrical *Diversion of Angels* (1948) and of *Adorations* (1975). There are three solos: *Lamentation* (1930), Medea's dance of vengeance from *Cave of the Heart* (1946) (both somewhat marred by closeups), and *Frontier* (1935). The film also includes another *Appalachian Spring*; a simultaneous projection of this film with the earlier version (filmed in 1958) can be extremely instructive about changes in Graham and her company (see pp. 48-50).

LAMENTATION, a cluster of camera perspectives made in 1943 of Graham in her famous solo, can also be compared with the performance on the 1975 film.

*Bettis.* Valerie Bettis' solo, THE DESPERATE HEART, a work from 1943, has been nicely filmed. Viewers would be helped if they had previously read the John Malcolm Brinnin poem that accompanies the dance. It is reprinted in Margaret Lloyd's *Borzoi Book of Modern Dance*.

*Tudor.* The expensive film, AMERICAN BALLET THEATRE: A CLOSE-UP IN TIME, features a magnificent full-length *Pillar of Fire* (1942) with Sallie Wilson as Hagar. A preliminary analysis of Tudor's approach and Arnold Schoenberg's music would be beneficial.

The availability of the above film increases the value of MODERN BALLET, an older film in which Tudor discusses his work while Hugh Laing and Nora Kaye (and, once, Tudor himself) demonstrate with excerpts. Like other segments of the "A Time to Dance" series, this film suffers from its transparently contrived conversational format, but the discussion is mostly valuable and the performances are mostly excellent—definitive, in fact. Kaye, Laing (who came out of retirement to make this film), and Tudor were all in the original cast of *Pillar of Fire* and the excerpts from that work on the film (the seduction of Hagar and a brief duet between Hagar and the Suitor) can be compared to the performances on the newer film. For example, one can see rather clearly how much more sharply etched is Laing's interpretation of the Man Across the Way than is Marcos Paredes', while Sallie Wilson's performance seems to hold up very well indeed, even in comparison with the legendary Nora Kaye.

*De Mille.* The first half of *Rodeo* (1942) is on the expensive AMERICAN BALLET THEATRE: A CLOSE-UP IN TIME, splendidly danced and with Christine Sarry in the lead role. The feature, CAROUSEL, has substantially preserved de Mille's effective dreamy ballet for that musical. Also available is a severely truncated and oddly photographed version of de Mille's 1948 ballet, FALL RIVER LEGEND (about which she has written a book), but

it is of little value and much the same can be said for AGNES DE MILLE'S A CHERRY TREE CAROL.

*Limón.* MOOR'S PAVANE, José Limón's masterpiece from 1949, can be seen in an abbreviated version. Much of the choreography for Emilia has been cut as has all the material after Desdemona's death. In addition, some portentously enunciated lines from Shakespeare have been needlessly superimposed by the filmmaker, mainly at the beginning and at the end. The film is still reasonably effective and offers definitive performances including that of Limón himself. Viewers of the film should be aware of the Othello story, of the significance of the handkerchief, of the way Limón filters the story through the courtly dance patterns, of the cuts on the film, and of Limón's superior judgment in not including the distracting Shakespearian oratory in the staged dance work.

Extensive excerpts from Limón's *There Is a Time* (1956) are performed on LANGUAGE OF DANCE, and a complete performance of his dramatic 1956 work EMPEROR JONES is available.

*Ross.* Herbert Ross' *Caprichos* (1949) is performed in full on DANCE—A REFLECTION OF OUR TIMES. The film also includes a conversation with the choreographer in which he discusses the Goya etchings on which his ballet is based. Slides of these etchings from the "Caprichos" collection (numbers 8, 9, 24, and 26) might be made to be shown separately and for greater length than they appear on the film. They can also be shown on a separate screen as the film is running. If one rehearses, it is possible to display them for the short periods in which they are quoted in the ballet without creating a distraction or ruining choreographic surprises.

*Balanchine.* Materials are still very limited. In the last twenty years, well over thirty of his ballets have been filmed and shown on television or in theaters but, for various reasons, the films now remain tucked away in archives in Berlin, Montreal, Paris, and New York.

An excellent available film is DANCE: NEW YORK CITY BALLET which includes works choreographed between 1957 and 1964: two complete Balanchine duets (*Tarantella* and *Meditation*) and excerpts from two others (*Agon* and *Tchaikovsky Pas de Deux*). Even this limited sampling helps to show the variety of the choreographer's work. (An interesting comparison with *Agon* can be arranged by scheduling a showing, at the same time, of the excerpts from Béjart's *Erotica* duet that appear on BALLET OF THE 20TH CENTURY. Béjart's choreography for Suzanne Farrell, who also dances the *Agon* material, seems to exploit her extraordinary abilities in a parade of shallow choreographic gimmicks and pointless discontinuities.)

There is a fine *Apollo* (1928) solo and some out-of-sync *Rubies* (1967) excerpts on BALLET WITH EDWARD VILLELLA, as well as more excerpts from the *Tchaikovsky Pas de Deux*. Melissa Hayden and Jacques d'Amboise perform a version of Balanchine's *Nutcracker Pas de Deux* on the 1960 film A TIME TO DANCE, and Maria Tallchief and Andre Eglevsky deliver the coda to his *Sylvia Pas de Deux* (1950) on CLASSICAL BALLET. A beautiful film of Balanchine's 1962 ballet MIDSUMMER NIGHT'S DREAM has been made but rentals are still very expensive and only the 35mm version is in Panavision (the 16mm version simply lops off the sides along with much of the choreography).

There is a good documentary on Balanchine's school, SCHOOL OF AMERICAN BALLET. And his rather impressive Hollywood choreography can be seen on the four features he completed there in the late 1930s and early 1940s (detailed on p. 73).

*Ashton.* An effective film of the superb 1968 ballet ENIGMA VARIATIONS is available. Also valuable are extensive and well-danced excerpts from Ashton's delightful *La Fille Mal Gardée* (1960) on BALLET FOR ALL—7.

A Fonteyn/Nureyev rehearsal of a beautiful duet from Ashton's *Birthday Offering* (1956) is on MARGOT FONTEYN. A movement from *Monotones II* (1965) is included on the film OPUS, and there is footage of Ashton rehearsing it on BEHIND THE SCENES WITH THE ROYAL BALLET. Ashton's choreography is also found on the often-impressive feature film, TALES OF HOFFMANN. The *La Valse* (1958) on EVENING WITH THE ROYAL BALLET is probably worth ignoring. A fine full-length *Ondine* (1958) with Fonteyn and Somes appears on ROYAL BALLET. There is a good performance of Ashton's *Marguerite and Armand* (1963) on the very expensive I AM A DANCER.

*Cullberg.* An excellent *Miss Julie* (1950) is on SWEDEN: FIRE AND ICE. As the film is being shown, some comments about Strindberg's play would be helpful as would a few elucidations of characters as they are not specifically identified on the film. Cullberg's discussion of the work in *Dance Perspectives* No. 29 is helpful.

*Sokolow.* Two works are available. Her 1955 study of alienation in the jazz age is on DANCE: ANNA SOKOLOW'S ROOMS and a more abstract work from 1965 is on ANNA SOKOLOW DIRECTS—ODES. The latter film includes some excellent rehearsal footage. Far less satisfactory is the documentary approach to *Opus 65* (1965) found in OPUS OP.

*Robbins.* No films are available. With rare exceptions Jerome Robbins has been strongly opposed to having his ballets seen in any format other than the intended live, theatrical one, although his works have been thoroughly filmed for record purposes.

*Tetley.* Ably represented on the free film, ANATOMY LESSON. The Rembrandt painting on which the ballet is based is shown briefly at the beginning and end of the film. A slide of the painting would allow more careful perusal. Comments by Tetley on the work are included in articles on the film in the June 1968 issue of *Dance and Dancers*.

*Petit.* Highly recommended is the superb Nureyev/Jeanmaire performance of YOUNG MAN AND DEATH (JEUNE HOMME ET LA MORT). The flashy, pretentious IN PRAISE OF FOLLY should be avoided.

*Béjart.* The BOLERO film is quite fine. BALLET OF THE 20TH CENTURY is rather fragmentary. There is some useful material available on videotape through CAMERA THREE.

*Joffrey/Arpino.* A good film, DANCE: ROBERT JOFFREY BALLET, gives some idea of what the company and its choreography were like in 1965. ATTITUDES IN DANCE shows two of Arpino's best works, *Ballet for Four* and *Sea Shadow*, beautifully performed. The rather poor film, OPUS OP, shows what it was like for the company to be "with it"—in 1967.

*Feld.* There is a fine documentary on the Eliot Feld of 1970, AMERICAN BALLET COMPANY, but no substantial examples of his choreography are available.

*Cunningham.* A good film of WALKAROUND TIME (1968) is available, but it is a very wry, spare, and understated work and, unless it is handled carefully, it may not be the best introduction to this important choreographer. The excerpts on A VIDEO EVENT, two programs done for CBS' *Camera Three*, are an excellent introduction (Part 2 is better than Part 1); they are available only on videotape. The color film of the first performance of RAINFOREST (1968) is fairly well done. Cunningham's video work, WESTBETH (1975), is a very engaging film, but the picture quality is rather poor. The short film, MERCE CUNNINGHAM, is an utter waste of time and money.

*Taylor.* The color documentary, PAUL TAYLOR AND COMPANY, is an attractive introduction to this choreographer and his dancers (as of 1968). The dance excerpts are maddeningly brief, but they do serve to illustrate the variety of Taylor's choreography. Taylor's JUNCTION, choreographed in 1961, is complete on film and is highly recommended.

*Nikolais.* A 1960 film, INVENTION IN DANCE, gives some indication of what this choreographer is up to—but it is not in color and that is a major loss in the case of Nikolais. While no color films portraying the company on stage are available, there are several filmic interpretations by Ed Emshwiller of the Nikolais approach. The best of these is FUSION.

*Louis.* Murray Louis has made an engaging, if overpriced, set of color films, DANCE AS AN ART FORM, that serve to give some indication of his choreographic approach. Of these the best is probably MOTION.

*Ailey.* Although the color definition on the film is often rather poor, ALVIN AILEY:MEMORIES AND VISIONS is popular with audiences. It is an excellent overview, though it is regrettable that only excerpts from his *Revelations* (1960) are included. (Two complete versions of *Revelations* have appeared on television, one from the early days of the company, another from more recent times; neither is available, it seems.) One movement from *The River* (1970) is well danced on the expensive film AMERICAN BALLET THEATRE:A CLOSE-UP IN TIME.

*Tharp.* A complete performance of the brilliant and witty *Sue's Leg* (1974) makes up the last half of the excellent film SUE'S LEG/REMEMBERING THE THIRTIES. Also of value: a performance of the 1971 work, THE BIX PIECES, on the *Camera Three* series, available only on videotape.

*Post-Cunningham.* Except for a good film of Kei Takei's haunting LIGHT, PART 5 (choreographed in 1971), works by members of what might be called the Post-Cunningham generation in modern dance are to date largely unavailable on film. Films and videotapes do exist, however, and may often be pried loose on an informal basis from the individual choreographers.

*Soviet ballet.* The extremely popular films, GALINA ULANOVA and, especially,PLISETSKAYA DANCES, are fine introductions to the subject. The brilliant profile of Maya Plisetskaya in George Feifer's book, *Our Motherland*, can be used to add depth about the dancer's personality and her position in Soviet society and politics. Lavrovsky's 1940 ballet, ROMEO AND JULIET (excerpted on the Ulanova and Plisetskaya films), is also available on a fairly adequate, more or less complete, version in color with Ulanova.

The two famous dancers appear together on an excellent half-hour version of Rostislav Zakharov's *Fountain of Bakhchisarai* (1934) which appears under the title SCENES FROM THE BALLET OF FOUNTAIN OF BAKHCHISARAI.

Various Soviet (and other) dancers appear on WORLD'S YOUNG BALLET which documents the 1969 Moscow ballet competition. (Among the winners shown: Mikhail Baryshnikov.) And RUSSIAN BALLET AND FOLK DANCES is certainly surefire, especially the exuberant dancing of the coal miners. Alberto Alonso's *Carmen* is performed on ALICIA.

*Chinese Ballet.* Represented by RED DETACHMENT OF WOMEN.

*Astaire.* Fred Astaire is the only important choreographer whose works have been precisely and thoroughly preserved and, as indicated in the directory, his features are readily rentable. Unfortunately, few of the dance episodes can be obtained separately, so one must take them plot and all. But having them on film allows one to go over the dance numbers repeatedly and that can be a fascinating experience. Arlene Croce's superb *Fred Astaire & Ginger Rogers Book* is an invaluable guide in any such exercise.

*Cine-dance.* The two cine-dance films that seem to work best with dance audiences are by Norman McLaren: the multiple images of PAS DE DEUX, and BALLET ADAGIO, a slow motion, somewhat revised version of Asaf Messerer's *Spring Water*.

Also recommended are the mistily romantic IN A REHEARSAL ROOM, and FUSION, the most engaging example of the Nikolais/Emshwiller collaborations. Hilary Harris' excellent NINE VARIATIONS ON A DANCE THEME seems most successful if one announces before each variation what film technique is to be applied (the filmmaker has provided a guide in his article in *Dance Perspectives* No. 30). Leni Riefenstahl's classic OLYMPIA DIVING SEQUENCE is a brilliant addition to any film program.

# Simultaneous projection

In the discussion above and in the notes in the directory below there are a number of suggestions about closely comparing two films, for example: two complete performances of *Appalachian Spring*, or different performances of duets from *Pillar of Fire* or *Swan Lake* or *Nutcracker*, or solos from *Sleeping Beauty* or *Don Quixote*, or various versions of *Dying Swan*.

These comparisons can be done sequentially, of course, but sometimes it can be quite enlightening to project the two films simultaneously using two different projectors. This would not be a good way to introduce someone to the dance work of course, but, for those already familiar with the work, simultaneous projection can point up similarities and subtle differences in a special and striking way. It requires a certain amount of ocular ping-pong from the viewer, but the eye and the brain seem generally able to cope successfully.

One way to handle this is to have the sound coming from the slower performance of the two films and to stop the faster performance from time to time, allowing the slower performance to catch up. Projectors will vary slightly in speed, too, so this should be taken into account.

If you plan to do such a screening for an audience, you should rehearse once or twice to attain projector stops that are as choreographically unobtrusive as possible.

## Some cautionary comments about videotape

Videotape is becoming increasingly important to dance. Some materials in this directory are available on videotape as well as on film. A few are available only on tape.

In addition many choreographers and dance companies are now making use of videotape as a seemingly inexpensive way to "preserve" their repertories. While this development is far preferable to relying entirely on memory to reconstruct or polish a work for performance, it can lead to a misguided complacency—the assumption that once the work is on videotape it can always be retrieved. In fact, *it should not be assumed that the picture recorded on videotape is permanent.*

How long a picture will last on videotape is a matter of conjecture—there seem to be no systematic studies of the issue, though some are in process. The major users of videotape are concerned only about short term preservation and makers of videotape have devoted themselves to supplying this need. In other words, videotape has simply not been designed as an archival medium, and manufacturers have given long-term considerations very little thought because few of their customers care about it.

It appears that the picture life depends on several variables—particularly on how the tapes are stored. In general, professional studio-type tapes (two-inch, quadraplex) are considered more reliable than the half-inch, helical-scan tapes in use by most amateurs. But one professional says that under ideal storage conditions his assumption is that his two-inch tapes will be good for no more than three years.

That is just a rule of thumb, of course. There is a good chance a tape will last longer than that. I recently played back a half-inch tape I made in 1971 and it looked fine. And one engineer I talked to said he had just finished reviewing a set of two-inch tapes that were up to ten years old and generally found them to be in good shape. By the same token, however, just about everyone—particularly those who have worked with half-inch tape—can relate personal horror stories of tapes that became unviewable within a year, a few months, or even days.

There are a number of things that can happen to a tape to make it unviewable (besides accidental erasure). For one, the tape can physically disintegrate—bits of it simply flake off. Where this happens the picture will show a momentary break-up. In addition, some of the dislodged flakes will imbed themselves in the playback heads of videotape recorders, thus clogging them. When this happens one must stop the machine and clean the heads. If this happens only occasionally, of course, it is a minor nuisance. But as the tape ages it can get worse and the tape can be rendered useless.

Also, the tape may stretch or contract so that the picture will no longer register. This seems to be a particular problem with half-inch and other helical-scan recorders where the picture information is laid out in long diagonals across the tape, and where the tape deck does not generally have compensating machinery built in.

Or the tape can become partially—or entirely—demagnetized by a passing magnetic field.

There is an additional problem, particularly with half-inch decks that may be lugged around a lot or that may not be kept in the best of repair. The deck may get out of calibration so that it produces a tape that will not be playable on a deck that *is* in calibration—or even on the original deck should its tuning degenerate further or be brought up to proper specifications in a repair shop.

Because of problems like these there are a number of procedures that are recommended for the most effective use of videotape. To begin with, the original taping should be on equipment that is in good repair, using brand new videotape, and in an environment that is as dust-free as possible. It would seem wise immediately to dub a backup tape (this requires two tape decks) and then store the two tapes in different places.

Always use a duplicate copy of a tape for rehearsal purposes—constant starting and stopping of a tape is very hard on it, leading to stretching and deterioration; also, tapes left threaded on a deck pick up and ingest dust from the air.

If there are any signs a tape is deteriorating, a duplicate should be made immediately. In all cases the tapes should be handled with great care, even if they are encased in a seemingly indestructible cassette.

*Storing videotapes.* There is some disagreement among sources about the best way to store videotape. All agree, however, that one should avoid subjecting the tape to extremes of, and rapid changes in, temperature and humidity.

Ideally the tape should be kept at a constant 70° F with fifty percent, relative humidity in a room that is air-conditioned with electrostatic filters. By manufacturer's standards videotape is reasonably hardy and can withstand temperature ranges of 60°-90° and relative humidity ranges of twenty percent-eighty percent. But to take the tape in and out of frigid temperatures or to let it bake in the trunk of a car is courting disaster. In fact, one authority says that temperature changes between 55° and 95° or humidity changes between ten percent and fifty percent *over a six month period* are almost guaranteed to cause trouble. The tape should also be stored in its protective case or encased in a plastic bag to keep out dust.

One should try to keep the tape away from magnetic fields. Advice on this score varies. Everyone agrees that tape should never be put close to (within three inches of) strong electric motors and some argue that, in addition, one should avoid storing it near fluorescent lights, television sets, loudspeakers, high intensity lamps, electrical transformers, electrical wiring (even if imbedded in a wall), or magnetic cabinet latches.

The tapes should be stored vertically so that the weight of the tape rests on the hub of the reel rather than the sides. This reduces edge wear on the tape which is also something one should be careful about when using the tape (make sure the feed and takeup reels are properly seated, never mash the sides of the reel together, etc.).

Some experts think it is a good idea to store the tape tails out (rewound before playing) since that produces a softer wind on the stored reel. Others think it's better to store the tapes tightly rewound on the reel. Others recommend yearly rewinding of the tape to shake it out.

*The alternative of film.* While recording a work on videotape is certainly far preferable to not recording it at all, it is clear that *serious archival recording of dance works should be done on film, not videotape.* Film today is extremely hardy—properly processed and stored it may well last as long as the finest paper: 700 years, or forever (whichever comes first).

Like videotape, film can be abused but, short of deliberate vandalism, the picture essentially is permanently affixed. Even if shrinkage eventually renders the film unprojectable, it still can be looked at on special viewers and can be reconstructed by re-photographing it or by procedures that stretch it into normal shape long enough for it to be duplicated. Even films that have been immersed in water can often be salvaged. And, of course, the picture on film is far clearer and more informative that anything on video.

The color on film, however, is not normally permanent. In ten or twenty years the color will often quite noticeably lose brilliance and one is usually left with an image that is pink-and-white (but at least there still is an image). Consequently black-and-white film, which gives a crisper picture anyway, is generally to be preferred for archival purposes.

Film stock costs much more than videotape. But the economies of videotape end there. Videotape equipment is far more expensive (and spends far more time in the repair shop) than film equipment. The costs of technical personnel, which are the major budget item in any serious recording effort, are much the same for either medium, but videotape editing can be phenomenally expensive.

For more detail on these issues, see "Preserving the Moving Image" by Ralph N. Sargent, available from Corporation for Public Broadcasting, 888 16 Street NW, Washington, DC 20006, for $3.95.

# Related materials

*Slide sets.* Attractive sets of dance slides, capably selected, well produced, and amply annotated, are available for various historical periods from Visual Resources, Inc., 1 Lincoln Plaza, New York, NY 10023, and from Pictura Dance, 25 W. 86 Street, New York, NY 10023.

*Other dance film catalogs.* David L. Parker and Esther Siegel, *Guide to Dance in Films* (1977), Gale Research Co., Book Tower, Detroit, MI 48226; *Catalog of Dance Films* (1974), Dance Films Association, 250 W. 57 Street, New York, NY 10019.

*Mailing list.* A mailing list of over 1000 dance film users with the names and addresses on pressure-sensitive labels is available for $30 from American Dance Guild, 152 W. 42 Street, New York, NY 10036.

# Up-to-date information; queries

New films become available all the time and this book, of course, is only as up-to-date as its time of publication. It is planned that updates to this directory will be put together from time to time. For a free copy, send a stamped, self-addressed envelope to

Addendum, Dance Film Archive, University of Rochester, Rochester, NY 14627.   No letter is necessary.

In addition I write a regular column for *Dance Magazine* that attempts to give current news and reviews of dance films.

If you have questions about the value or availability of a ballet or modern dance film, please feel free to write me at Dance Film Archive, University of Rochester, Rochester, NY 14627.   Please enclose a stamped, self-addressed envelope.   No guarantees, but I'll try to help.

J.M.

# Directory

## Films on ballet and modern dance

ACROBATS OF GOD. 22 min., 1969, color.**

*Rental $9.80 from Minnesota, $11.60 from Illinois, $20 from Budget, $25 from Pyramid. Sale $300 from Pyramid.*

Martha Graham's comic vision of the creative process, choreographed in 1960. Graham, as the choreographer (helped by Robert Powell as the whip-toting regisseur), mulls over a parade of choreographic ideas, some lyrical, some frenetic, many parodic, presented to her by the dancers. At the end, she is ready to begin the composition.

Music by Carlos Surinach, setting by Isamu Noguchi. Adapted for the camera by John Butler, directed by Dave Wilson. The color quality is somewhat faded. For photographs of what Graham really looks like when creating a new work, see Leroy Leatherman, *Martha Graham*, pp. 52-53. Also appearing on the film are Mary Hinkson, Helen McGehee, Takako Asakawa, Phyllis Gutelius, Noemi Lapzeson, Bertram Ross, Robert Cohan, Clive Thompson, William Louther, and Robert Dodson.

ADAGIO (L'ADAGE). 14 min., 1963, b/w.*

*Rental $12 from FACSEA, $15 from Radim. Sale $125 from Radim.*

A hauntingly successful film commentary on the dancer and on the romance of the ballet adagio. At the Paris Opéra, Nina Vyroubova and Attilio Labis wind into and out of material from *Giselle* Act II.

ADOLESCENCE. 22 min., 1966, b/w.*

*Rental $7.60 from Illinois, $8.75 from Indiana, $9 from South Florida, $12.50 from Syracuse, $14 from California, $15 from Audio Brandon. Sale $150 from Audio Brandon.*

A Parisian schoolgirl takes lessons from the aged Madame Lubov Egorova and auditions for a ballet company. Directed by Vladimir Forgency.

AFTERNOON OF A FAUN. 10 min., 1952. X

The film featuring Liselotte Koester and Jockel Stahl is apparently no longer available.

AFTERNOON OF A FAUN. 11 min., 1973, color.*

*Rental $11, sale $160 from Rochester.*

An attempt at an approximate reconstruction of the choreography of Nijinsky's famous version of this ballet. Scores of still photographs and drawings from the original performances by Nijinsky are coordinated with the Debussy score following the description of the ballet given in Richard Buckle's *Nijinsky*. Occasional subtitles are used to explain the action. Gives an idea of the shape of the choreography and of Nijinsky's strange stage presence. The Leon Bakst designs for the ballet are also shown, in color. Directed by John Mueller. See also BALLET FOR ALL—6: BALLET COMES TO BRITAIN.

AGNES DE MILLE'S A CHERRY TREE CAROL. 9 min., 1975, color.

*Rental $6.45 from Northern Illinois, $7 from Illinois, $7.25 from Minnesota, $9 from Syracuse. Sale $160 from ACI.*

This brief, rather bland ballet, originally produced for educational television in 1971, tells the story of the popular folk Christmas carol about a miracle in which a cherry tree bends down to offer its fruit to the expectant Virgin Mary. The dancers are in pioneer garb and the choreography resembles a mellowed imitation of *Appalachian Spring* in style.

The dancers are students from the North Carolina School of the Arts with school dean, Robert Lindgren, appearing as Joseph. Director/photographer Gardner Compton has chosen to festoon the piece with dissolves and overlapping exposures in an apparent attempt to generate more visual interest than the choreography provides.

AIR FOR THE G STRING. 7 min., 1934, b/w.**

*Rental $5 from Illinois, $8 from Rochester. Sale from Dance Films.*

Doris Humphrey and a group of four in a beautifully filmed version of her early dance work, choreographed in 1928. Portions seem a bit out of sync. The other dancers are Cleo Atheneos, Dorothy Lathrop, Ernestine Stodelle, and Hyla Rubin.

Humphrey had not danced in the original choreography herself, but took the lead for the making of this film. The film includes some exquisite closeups of the choreographer.

AIR FOR THE G STRING

ALICIA. 69 min., 1976, color, cinemascope (special, anamorphic lens required for projector—see p. 6). Also available in 35mm.*

*Rental $200 ($100 classroom). Sale $950 from Tricontinental.*

An entertaining Cuban-made documentary on the great ballerina Alicia Alonso. About three-quarters of the film is devoted to dancing by Alonso and the National Ballet of Cuba. The rest is given over to a flashy, portentous sketch of Alonso's extraordinary career (using stills and newspaper clippings), to some rehearsal and classroom scenes, and to an interview with the ballerina.

In the first half of the film three items from classics are inserted: tantalizing excerpts from Act I of *Giselle* (Giselle's entrance and a later solo), a complete *Black Swan Pas de Deux* (partnered confi-

dently by Azari Plisetski), and portions of the satiric *Pas de Quatre* with Alonso soloing in the Taglioni role. These three segments, all in black and white, were shot in the mid-1960s when Alonso was in her mid-forties. By the standards that prevail in New York at present, they are taken at rather slow tempos. But this allows plenty of time for Alonso to articulate the drama she feels in the characterization and in the music, and for her to hold endlessly her firm balances. And it certainly does not keep her from dashing off a dazzling set of perfectly controlled pirouettes or fouettés when she feels like it.

The last half hour of the film is taken up with a complete, or nearly complete, performance of Alberto Alonso's *Carmen*, filmed in the mid-1970s in color. There is a lot of heavy conceptualization in this ballet; the work ends, for example, with a double duet which concludes as the bull (danced by a sleek ballerina with a fierce expression on her face) dies at the same time as Carmen. But Alonso almost makes the title role believable as she delivers with a certain fiery conviction the naively sexual hip thrusts, the unflinching come-hither-if-you-dare stares, and the pointlessly eccentric crossed-ankle steps.

Alonso proves to be as beautiful in closeups in the interviews as she is in long shot in the dancing sequences, and somehow she even manages to fashion arresting answers to some of the inane questions fired at her (in Spanish, with English subtitles) by an off-camera interviewer: "Alicia, what is the hardest part about dancing?" "Dancing well." She also discusses, candidly and touchingly, her near-blindness.

Alonso has remained in Cuba since 1959, loyal to the Castro regime (as the narration stresses), and some of the stills show that she has appeared in at least one of those "revolutionary" ballets—all clenched fists and clutched rifles and clichéd grimaces.

ALVIN AILEY—MEMORIES AND VISIONS. 54 min., 1975, color.**

*Rental $24 from Illinois, $50 from Budget, $75 from Phoenix. Sale $750 from Phoenix (film or videotape cassette).*

Ailey's company dances excerpts from his works on the program, originally produced in 1974 for Public Broadcasting Service. For some reason the transfer from videotape did not work out very well; there is often a problem of fuzzy focus and the color definition is quite poor in sections where there is a lot of yellow or orange. Nonetheless, the film is always viewable and effective and is extremely successful with audiences.

The program concludes with fourteen minutes of *Revelations*, Ailey's moving and highly effective work to a set of spirituals. The sections chosen—"Wading in the Water" and its processional, and the closing numbers—reflect only the "up" side of the work. The other side, reflected in numbers like "Fix Me, Jesus," "I Want to be Ready," and "Sinner Man," is not shown. Instead, there are excerpts from other Ailey works: two sections of *Blues Suite*; excerpts from *Lark Ascending* (with Sara Yarborough at her splendid, and usual, best); four excerpts from *Mary Lou's Mass*; "Right On, Be Free," the concluding section of the solo work, *Cry*, with Judith Jamison; *A Song for You*, a solo for Dudley Williams; and sections of *Hidden Rites*. The dancing by the Ailey company is uniformly excellent, as is the direction of Stan Lathan.

Judith Jamison in ALVIN AILEY—MEMORIES AND VISIONS

In a mostly on-camera commentary that is reminiscent of detective fiction ("I'm Alvin Ailey. I'm a choreographer. I create movement."), Ailey introduces the numbers and tells us about things that have influenced him. If the film seems somewhat too long for a classroom hour, one might begin it after Ailey's introduction (he repeats it all later anyway).

Other dancers on the film include Nerissa Barnes, Masazumi Chaya, Ulysses Dove, Melvin Jones, Mari Kajiwara, Linda Kent, Edward Love, Hector Mercado, Christa Mueller, Michichiko Oka, John Parks, Kenneth Pearl, Kelvin Rotardier, Dana Sapiro, Estelle Spurlock, Clive Thompson, Sylvia Waters, Elbert Watson, Donna Wood, Peter Woodin, and Tina Yuan.

## AMERICAN BALLET COMPANY—ELIOT FELD, ARTISTIC DIRECTOR. 58 min., 1971, color.*

*Rental $60, sale $600 from Blackwood Productions, Inc., 58 W. 58 Street, NYC 10019; (212) 688-0930.*

A highly effective documentary on the beginnings of Eliot Feld's first company. The company was born in 1969; cameras were there to record auditions, rehearsals, background turmoil, anxieties over funding, and the first major performances at Spoleto, Italy.

The photographers were around enough so that the dancers became accustomed to their presence. The result is some extraordinary footage capturing moments of tension and of relaxation, of exuberance and of desperation. At the center is an agonizing rehearsal which Feld abruptly leaves in a moment of utter frustration. One camera crew remains with the dancers recording their depression and bewilderment, while another follows Feld to a coffee shop where he expatiates on his reactions, dejectedly perceiving and admitting his own "bad criticism" in the rehearsal, his own "self-indulgence."

The film should be taken as a historical document. Feld's American Ballet Company collapsed in 1971 and was succeeded in 1974 by the present company, the Eliot Feld Ballet. But it was in those times, in the moods and conditions shown in the film, that Feld produced what so far has proven to be his best choreography. However good the film is at portraying human relationships, it shows little of Feld's choreography, although there are glimpses of *At Midnight*, *Intermezzo*, and *The Consort* on stage or in rehearsal. So we have an excellent documentary showing Eliot Feld screaming at his dancers, but no companion film to show the ballets the screaming produced.

Among the dancers shown are Christine Sarry, Richard and Cristina Munro, Elizabeth Lee, John Sowinski, Olga Janke, and Alfonso Figueroa.

## AMERICAN BALLET THEATRE: A CLOSE-UP IN TIME. 90 min., 1973, color.**

*Rental $150 for one to three showings from Arthur Cantor, Inc., 234 W. 44 Street, NYC 10036; (212) 391-0450.*

A complete performance, brilliantly photographed, of Antony Tudor's *Pillar of Fire* with Sallie Wilson as Hagar is featured. (Excerpts from this work, danced by the roles' creators, also appear on MODERN BALLET, and can provide an interesting comparison—see p. 51).) In addition, the film includes a staging of the *Black Swan Pas de Deux* by David Blair danced by Cynthia Gregory and Ted Kivitt, the first movement from Michel Fokine's *Les Sylphides*, the first half of Agnes de Mille's *Rodeo* featuring the sparkling Christine Sarry, the "Lake" section of Alvin Ailey's *The River*, and the "Tarantella" from Harald Lander's *Etudes*. Interview material with de Mille, Tudor, Lucia Chase, and some of the dancers is also included.

This superb program, originally created for public television, was put together as a kind of tribute to ABT, showing the range of the company's repertory. Director Jerome Schnur has done an excellent job. To envelop the action he likes to use a single, choreographed camera that roams widely—an approach similar to Fred Astaire's—rather than a lot of cuts from one camera to another. However, the camera positions are generally out front where the audience would be and the choreography is substantially unaltered so one still gets a good feel for how the ballets look on the stage.

The camera is allowed to journey behind the dancers only in two sequences: the opening—the last movement of *Les Sylphides* with Karena Brock, Sarry, Ellen Everett, and John Prinz—where shots from (specially-constructed) wings are intended to convey the theatrical nature of the enterprise; and in the section of *The River* (featuring Gregory and Marcos Paredes) where the swirling and somewhat disorienting camera work seems singularly appropriate.

Schnur relies heavily on a wide-angle lens to get the fullest view and to minimize focusing problems. (However, for some reason the picture is never in absolutely crisp focus in the dance portions of the film, an effect that may be somewhat more noticeable, and objectionable to some viewers, on the big screen.) The wide-angle lens tends to exaggerate distances so that upstage dancers appear farther away and hence smaller than they would to the eye. On television this sometimes resulted in distant dancers looking tiny to the point of insignificance; on the big screen, however, they are quite large enough and the vastness of the space defined by Schnur's camera is, at least in this case, most inviting.

The film's finest half hour is the *Pillar of Fire* section. At an open meeting in 1973, Tudor expressed great satisfaction with the video recording. He had approached the project with misgivings, he said, due to some earlier unhappy experiences with television, but he soon found the director "knew more about *Pillar* than I did" and was entirely sensitive to the ballet's needs. Schnur, in fact, is a great admirer of Tudor's works and was determined to do justice to this masterpiece. He has succeeded brilliantly. Wilson

gives a standard-setting performance and she is supported by Gayle Young as the Suitor, Marcos Paredes as the Man Across the Way, Bonnie Mathis as the Older Sister, and Ellen Everett as the Younger Sister.

Another highlight is the scene from *Rodeo*. Schnur's wide open spaces work particularly well in this case, and the ballet's juxtaposition to *Pillar of Fire* is of interest since both works approach, in very different ways, a similar psychological theme.

Cynthia Gregory is seen to fine effect both in *The River* section and, representing ABT's classical wing, in the *Black Swan Pas de Deux*. The duet seems oddly vacant without an audience of ecstatic fans. The decision to clutter the floor with a large imprinted design does not make viewing much easier.

The program concludes with the Tarantella finale of *Etudes* (featuring Ivan Nagy, Kivitt, and Eleanor D'Antuono). In this case photographing the cluttering floor design is highly detrimental to the effect, even in big screen viewing. The camera also seems to be placed too low most of the time in this ballet.

The transfer from videotape to film (by Image Transform of New York) is easily the best on any available dance film. There is a problem with the film (besides its high rental rate): it is variably in and out of sync. Because funds were limited the dancers were originally videotaped performing to piano music. Then efforts were made to get additional money to hire an orchestra. The conductor, Akira Endo, who had also been the pianist in the original, then had the task of matching the orchestra to his piano music. The orchestral performances are quite good, but Endo was incapable of obtaining a perfect match with the piano original. The mismatch is by no means bad enough to negate the film's substantial virtues; and too much concern about the issue can ruin one's enjoyment of the film. But sharp-eyed (and -eared) viewers may be set to wondering from time to time about what seem to be lapses in the dancers' musicality, and they should know where the blame lies. One other problem: there is occasionally a small strobe-like effect in the picture, a very minor distraction.

ANATOMY LESSON. 25 min., 1968, color.**

*Rental free from Association (ask for film no. L-722).*

A highly effective production of the Glen Tetley work which explores, in a series of flashbacks, the tormented past of the man on the dissecting table in Rembrandt's painting.

The excellent dancing is by the Netherlands Dance Theater, headed by Jaap Flier, with Willy de la Bije as his Mother, Alexandra Radius as his Wife, and Ger Thomas as the Doctor. The music is by Marcel Landowsky. A joint production of British and Dutch television, the film was produced by Margaret Dale of the BBC and first shown in Britain in 1968. For a discussion of the work and the television production and an interview with the producer, see *Dance and Dancers*, June 1968.

ANN, A PORTRAIT. 24 min., 1973, color.

*Rental $30, sale $275 from Time-Life.*
An impressionistic film by Constance Beeson on San Francisco's Ann Halprin. See also HALPRIN and PROCESSION.

ANNA SOKOLOW DIRECTS—ODES. 40 min., 1972, b/w.*

*Rental $12.50 from Ohio State, $12.50 from Illinois. Sale $320 from Ohio State.*
The choreographer was filmed in 1966 at Ohio State University preparing students for a technique demonstration and teaching them *Odes*, a work choreographed in 1965 to the music of Edgard Varèse. An excellent performance by Ohio State's University Dance Group of this twenty-one-minute, three-movement work concludes the film (with the duet danced by James Payton and Susannah Newman).

The camera work loses quite a bit of the shape of the dance work by concentrating too closely on the intensity of the individual movement, but the impact of this powerfully unsettling dance composition still comes through effectively. The rehearsal scenes are excellent and serve to document Sokolow's approach to movement and theater. Directed by David Parker. A lively article on the Sokolow residency by one of the dancers, Senta Driver, appears in *Dance Scope*, Fall 1966.

APPALACHIAN SPRING. 31 min., 1958, b/w.**

*Rental $8 from South Florida, $9.40 from Michigan, $9.60 from Iowa, $9.90 from Illinois, $11 from Penn State, $11.50 from Indiana, $12 from Syracuse, $15 from Audio Brandon, $18 from California, $25 from Phoenix. Sale $250 from Phoenix.*
Martha Graham's masterful rendering of frontier hopes and fears, ably filmed by Peter Glushanok. Music by Aaron Copland, sets by Isamu Noguchi. Graham is the wife, Stuart Hodes the husband, Bertram Ross the preacher, Matt Turney the pioneer woman, and Yuriko, Helen McGehee, Ethel Winter, and Miriam Cole the worshippers.

Another version of the dance work was made in 1976 using a different cast. A side-by-side comparison of the two films is fascinating. For a discussion, see the notes for MARTHA GRAHAM DANCE COMPANY.

ART AND TECHNIQUE OF THE BALLET. 11 min.

*Rental $12.50 from Audio Brandon.*
A German documentary on ballet technique. Rehearsal of a Swan Lake quartet.

ART IS. 28 min., color.

*Rental free from Association (ask for film no. S-503).*
Includes brief sequences of Edward Villella in Balanchine's *Tchaikovsky Pas de Deux* and of Jerome Robbins talking about dance and rehearsing Patricia McBride and Helgi Tomasson in his *Goldberg Variations*. Also a segment on the mime, Tony Montanaro.

ASSEMBLAGE. 59 min., 1968, color.

*Rental $75, sale $750 from Film Wright, 4530 18 Street, San Francisco, CA 94114; (415) 863-6100.*
A film made in collaboration with Richard Moore of KQED, involving the Merce Cunningham Dance Company performing in Ghirardelli Square, San Francisco. Rather heavier on snappy camera work than on dance.

ATTIC SONGS. 15 min., 1975, color.

*Rental $25, sale $250 from E. J. Clark Films, 17335 Mierow Lane, Brookfield, WI 53005.*
Multiple images of dancing figure (Susie Bauer) and body parts. Dull.

ATTITUDES IN DANCE. 28 min., 1964, b/w.**

*Rental $16 from Rochester.*
The original casts from the Robert Joffrey Ballet Company and the Norman Walker Dance Company perform works by Gerald Arpino and Walker. Arpino is represented by *Ballet for Four* (Rieti) danced by Lisa Bradley, Lawrence Rhodes, Paul Sutherland, and Nels Jorgenson; and by *Sea Shadow* (Ravel) danced by Bradley and Sutherland. Walker is seen dancing his *Courtly Duet* (Vivaldi) with Cora Cahan and they are joined for his *Dance Finale* (Hovhaness) by Dale Best, Lynn Weinman, Marsha Wolfson, Bruce Becker, Jane Kosminsky, and Jeff Phillips. Beautifully photographed by Merrill Brockway.

BAGGAGE. 22 min., 1969, b/w.

*Rental $7.20 from Minnesota, $7.60 from Illinois, $8 from Penn State, $12 from Syracuse, $15 from Pyramid. Sale $160 from ACI.*
Features dancer Mamako Yoneyawa.

## BALANCHINE BALLET FILMS (CANADA). ?

Between 1957 and the 1970s the New York City Ballet performed at least seventeen Balanchine works for the Canadian Broadcasting Corporation in Montreal, most of them very simply, but quite effectively, filmed. There have been some efforts to get these programs released on film, so far without success. Inquiries should be directed to Laurier Hébert, CBC, P.O. Box 6000, Montreal H3C 3A8. Among these films are *Serenade* (filmed in 1957); *Apollo* (d' Amboise), *Orpheus*, and *Agon* (1960); *Liebeslieder Walzer* and *Divertimento No. 15* (1961); *Four Temperaments* and *Ivesiana* (1964); *Concerto Barocco*, *Divertimento Brilliante*, and *Apollo* (Martins) (1969); and *Tarantella*, *Movements*, and *Who Cares?* (1971).

## BALANCHINE BALLET FILMS (GERMANY). ?

In 1973 the New York City Ballet went to Germany to film fifteen Balanchine works. Many of these films, produced by Reiner Moritz, have been shown on U.S., Canadian, and European television, but none is yet available for rental or purchase on film. One of these, *Symphony in C*, directed by Joes Odufré (and by George Balanchine), is quite an excellent film. Most (or all?) of the others have been directed (mainly by Hugo Niebeling and Klaus Lindemann) so maniacally that the choreography is all but submerged.
The films include *Agon*, *Pulcinella*, *Stravinsky Violin Concerto*, *Duo Concertant*, *Liebeslieder Walzer*, *La Valse*, *Serenade*, *Tchaikovsky Pas de Deux*, *Episodes*, *Tarantella*, *Baiser de la Fée*, *Valse Fantaisie*, *Concerto Barocco*, and *Stars and Stripes*. For information about the films, contact Louis H. Powell, 130 W. 57 Street, NYC 10019; (212) 582-1122.

## BALLERINA (also known as POOR LITTLE BALLERINA and DREAM BALLERINA). 81 min., 1950, b/w.*

*Rental $60 ($48 classroom) from Ivy Film, 165 W. 46 Street, NYC 10036; (212) 765-3940 (higher for large audiences or when admission is charged).*

A fantasy feature film starring Violette Verdy. The film is bright and rather delicate, charming and well-paced, engaging and unusually imaginative. And it contains a great deal of brilliant dancing by a very remarkable young dancer. It might form an alternative, even an antidote, to the often-shown RED SHOES.

The plot of BALLERINA is light and mostly understated—no leaden melodrama here. Verdy, sixteen years old when the film was made, plays the role of a wide-eyed, innocent, rather intensely virginal dancer making her debut. The performance is a failure. Three men show an interest in her: a theater manager who wants her as his mistress, a jeweler who wants her as his wife, and a young jewel thief who dazzles her with compliments but who really wants to use her as an alibi for a robbery. Each of the three men inspires a lengthy choreographed dream for her that night. After the dreams the ultimate disillusionment with the young flatterer matures her, which leads to her success as a dancer.

The film was directed by Ludwig Berger and the choreography, mostly clean, simple, and quite effective, was supervised by Yvonne Georgi, the prominent German choreographer, dancer, and partner of Harald Kreutzberg. Berger had a long and distinguished career as a director, his most highly regarded films being the semi-fantastical *Cinderella* and *The Waltz Dream* produced at the famous Ufa studios during the 1920s, the heyday of German expressionism in films.

It is this bent for fantasy that he brings to the BALLERINA film and, since he has arranged the film to consist mostly of three danced dreams, he is able to let his imagination roam. In the first of the young dancer's dreams she sees herself taken to Paris as the theater manager's mistress; in the second she envisions a tempestuous married life with the jeweler; and in the third she goes to meet the young gangster on a bridge which leads, improbably, to a Spanish church wedding and an idyllic home life. Throughout, images and characters jumble, but Berger is careful to keep the fantasy perspective that of the rather bewildered young girl who is having the dreams.

To play the young gangster Berger had originally picked a male dancer from the Paris Opéra who was also an accomplished actor. However, in the final auditions, Verdy was chosen for the lead over a Paris Opéra ballerina and, according to the dictates of French ballet politics, this meant Berger could use no Paris Opéra dancers in his film. Accordingly, the role of the young man was elaborated. There is an acting character (Phillipe Nicaud) while the dancing is capably handled by Nicolas Orloff, who currently is a ballet teacher in New York. This device leads to some minor confusion in the film's plot, but since anything can happen in a dream, the confusion is fairly unimportant.

One of the film's greatest virtues is the choice of music to accompany its elaborate dream ballets. Instead of the usual clangorous third-rate film score, the dream ballets are danced to selections from Maurice Ravel. The film was originally shot in both English and French versions. It is the English version that is available.

## BALLERINA. 94 min., 1966, color.

*Rental $50 from any of the following: Association, Audio Brandon, Films Inc., ROA, Select.*

A Walt Disney feature about a girl's life and ambitions at the Royal Danish Ballet. Moments from Bournonville's *La Sylphide* and from the Russian classics are shown. Features Kirsten Simone.

## BALLET ADAGIO. 10 min., 1971, color.**

*Rental $5.50 from Kent State, $5.80 from Michigan, $6.50 from Indiana, $6.85 from Minnesota, $7 from Illinois, $8.50 from South Florida, $10 from Syracuse, $12.50 from Budget, $13 from Rochester, $20 from Pyramid. Sale $175 from Pyramid.*

A beautiful film by Canadian filmmaker Norman McLaren (see also his PAS DE DEUX). Highly successful with audiences. Asaf Messerer's show-stopping lyric duet, *Spring Water*, danced in minimal costumes by Canadian artists David and Anna-Marie Holmes, is filmed in slow motion (one-quarter speed). The technique makes possible almost a muscle-by-muscle analysis of the performance which would show glaringly any imperfections in it, but the continuity and the sensuousness of the dancers' adagio are preserved and savored.

Otherwise, the film work is very simple. The cameras are out front where the audience would be. There is some cutting between longer and closer shots, all from one angle, but very little zooming. The dancers are almost always kept fully in the frame. The choreography has been somewhat rearranged by Mr. Holmes and Messerer's Sergei Rachmaninoff music has been replaced by some flowing music for organ and strings usually attributed to Tomaso Albinoni (though it is probably by Giazotto).

For a good documentary on the lives of the two BALLET ADAGIO dancers (showing, among other things, grueling rehearsals for this film), see TOUR EN L'AIR.

David and Anna-Marie Holmes in BALLET ADAGIO

## BALLET BY DEGAS. 6 min., 1951, color.

*Rental $5 from Syracuse, $6 from Boston, $6.75 from Illinois, $11 from Audio Brandon. Sale $150 from Audio Brandon.*

Camera studies of ballet paintings.

## BALLET CONCERT. 55 min., 1951, b/w.*

*Rental $35, sale from Audio Brandon.*

A compilation of short films from Russia, apparently made during the Second World War. Presumably for morale purposes, most of them reflect the ballet of Leningrad which was under siege at the time.

1) *Waltz of the Flowers* played by orchestra with flitting corps; 2) a young Galina Ulanova in a version of the *Dying Swan*; 3) Vakhtang Chabukiani in pyrotechnics from *Taras Bulba*; 4) Olga Lepeshinskaya in variations from Act I of *Don Quioxte*; 5) Ulanova and Konstantin Sergeyev in three-quarters of the *Swan Lake* Act II adagio, performed without corps; 6) some energetic balalaika playing; 7) *Quadrille* by the Moiseyev Dancers; 8) a novelty duet, *Skating Rink*, featuring Anna Redel and Mikhail Krustalev; 9) a frolic for Lepeshinskaya and Rudenko; 10, 11, 12) three Moiseyev dances from Moldavia, Byelorussia, and Azerbaizhan; 13) Marina Semyonova and corps in some sort of choreography from *Swan Lake*; 14) Natalia Dudinskaya, Chabukiani, and corps in parts of the Shades scene from *Bayaderka*. Some of these are available separately: 13 under SWAN LAKE; 14 under BAYADERKA; 4, 5, and 6 are on RUSSIAN BALLET AND FOLK DANCES.

## BALLET FOR ALL: SEVEN BALLET HISTORY FILMS.*

This series of films features Ballet for All, an off-shoot of the Royal Ballet, founded in 1964 by Peter Brinson. The group, a mobile touring company, was created to bring ballet of good quality to all corners of Great Britain: some half dozen dancers, selected from among the younger members of the parent company, are accompanied by a couple of pianists and an actor-narrator to present a series of carefully devised lecture-demonstrations with minimal sets, but in full costume.

In 1970 some of this experience was packed into seven half-hour programs and presented on Thames Television. The programs, written by Brinson, are designed to give an introductory overview of the history of ballet (as seen from London) from Louis XIV to Frederick Ashton. The programs are a well-paced blend of narration, most of it delivered by the late David Blair, and a considerable variety of dance excerpts, many of them quite substantial and almost all of them well danced. Among the dancers are David Wall, Doreen Wells, Nicholas Johnson, Brenda Last, Margaret Barbieri, Deanne Bergsma, Alfreda Thorogood, Graham Usher, and Blair himself.

The bulk of the time is given over to dancing; talking heads make up only a small portion of each program. However, to compress everything into the limited time available, there is a considerable amount of narrative voice-over during most of the dance segments. This narration does go on too long at times and Blair proves to be a somewhat uncomfortable narrator. But what is related is generally informative and to the point, if sometimes a bit glib. Brinson seems to have a certainty about historic turning points and about stylistic differences that could use qualification and modification at times.

Of course Brinson does not represent the series to be the definitive word on ballet history. And, as the introduction it was intended to be, it is very serviceable indeed. Ballet schools may want to book the entire series to give students some idea of the tradition they represent. People teaching or interested in dance history may find in many of the programs valuable materials on which to build.

The dancing takes place before pleasant, unpretentious settings by Norman Garwood designed to preserve a stage feeling. Nicholas Ferguson's direction is quiet and unobtrusive—in a word, excellent. The lighting, apparently typical for British television, is somewhat inept. The music is provided by a piano supported here and there by a solo string instrument. Some of the programs were originally in color, but the transfer has been to black and white film for all of them. The transfer is of good quality though some programs have a slight, unobjectionable green cast to them.

Rental and purchase information for each film is given below. The set of seven can be purchased as a whole for $2360 from Heritage.

BALLET FOR ALL—1: HOW BALLET BEGAN. 26 min., 1970, b/w.

*Rental $13 from Illinois. Sale $340 from Heritage.*
Offers a breezy discussion of the development of ballet from its beginnings in royal European courts through the early nineteenth century.

Mary Skeaping has provided some choreography to illustrate *Ballet de la Nuit* (1653) with Louis XIV as the Sun, John Weaver's *Loves of Mars and Venus* (1716), and a shepherdess dance from Jean Georges Noverre's *Petits Riens* (1778). Of these the Weaver portions look the most probable. The excerpts are danced by Sven Bradshaw, Jacqueline Lansley, and Marion Tait. The segment concludes with approximately six minutes from Bournonville's *Konservatoriet* (1849) capably, though not definitively, danced

by Anthony Molyneux, Alison Howard, Anthony Rudenko, Tait, and Bradshaw. For contrast, the program begins with the last part of the adagio of the *Sleeping Beauty Pas de Deux* (Doreen Wells, David Wall) and part of the duet from Kenneth MacMillan's *Concerto* (Patricia Ruanne, Kerrison Cooke).

BALLET FOR ALL—2: BALLET ENTERS THE WORLD STAGE. 28 min., 1970, b/w.*

*Rental $14 from Illinois. Sale $340 from Heritage.*
Presents *Giselle* in a version for four dancers, one piano, and one viola. Danced excerpts include the opening scene, the courting scene, the accusation and mad scenes, Giselle's initiation, Albrecht's visit to the grave and duet with Giselle, and the concluding eleven minutes.

The charms of the ballet are different and perhaps more private in this chamber version, without either the bustle of the peasants or the ominous drillwork of the Wilis, and with Adolphe Adam's score rendered tinkly by a piano. It may take some getting used to, but the dancing, by Margaret Barbieri and Nicholas Johnson with Marion Tait as Myrtha and Fergus Early as Hilarion, is quite good. At times the narration becomes rather obtrusive, however. A discussion of various stylistic, thematic, and costume developments (including pointe work) and of conventionalized mime language is included. Also shown: the Sylph's opening dance from Bournonville's *La Sylphide* (Bridget Taylor).

BALLET FOR ALL—3: HOW BALLET WAS SAVED. 29 min., 1970, b/w.*

*Rental $14 from Illinois. Sale $340 from Heritage.*
Compares *Coppélia* as danced today (Brenda Last and Nicholas Johnson) with the original version of 1870 using a woman in the role of Franz (Janet Francis and Margaret Barbieri). The style of the 1870 version, coy and fussy, is based on the memories of Paulette Dynalix who was the last to dance the travesty Franz in the version maintained at the Paris Opéra until 1961. Several generous portions of the ballet—mime scenes and danced duets—are presented along with extended discussions of stylistic differences, ballet training, and the male role (or lack thereof) in ballet of the era.

Also seen: Alison Howard and Spencer Parker (betrothal dance) and the company's ballet master, Oliver Symons, as Dr. Coppélius. For valuable commentary, see Ivor Guest, *The Two Coppélias*.

BALLET FOR ALL—4: TCHAIKOVSKY AND THE RUSSIANS. 27 min., 1970, b/w.*

*Rental $13 from Illinois. Sale $340 from Heritage.*
Presents a comparison of Petipa and Ivanov with an

extended discussion of Ivanov's portions of *Swan Lake*, particularly stressing the use of swan motifs and the development of a special dance-mime language.

With the dancers demonstrating in the classroom, a blow-by-blow analysis of the famous Act II adagio is given, emphasizing its built-in imagery and its dramatic progression. Then the complete adagio is danced in costume (and without voice-over) by Doreen Wells and David Wall. For contrast, Wells and Wall dance the adagio from the aristocratic *Sleeping Beauty Pas de Deux* and Brenda Last and Alan Hooper render the coda of the *Bluebird Pas de Deux*. There are also some film clips of the Bolshoi corps in action in *Swan Lake*, Act IV.

BALLET FOR ALL—5: THE BEGINNINGS OF TODAY. 27 min., 1970, b/w.*

*Rental $13 from Illinois. Sale $340 from Heritage.*
A survey of Fokine and early Diaghilev, and of Anna Pavlova.

The waltz pas de deux from *Les Sylphides* (danced by Shirley Grahame and Graham Usher) is contrasted in style with portions of the *Swan Lake* and *Sleeping Beauty* duets. Usher also performs the male solo from *Les Sylphides*. Two portions of *Petrouchka*, fairly well danced, are then shown with accompanying discussion: the opening dance for the puppets and the complete Moor's cell scene (Usher and Grahame with Peter Clegg as the Blackamoor).

Pavlova's career and influence are discussed and she is shown in portions of two solos: *La Nuit* and *Dying Swan* (with orchestra dubbed later). This is the only available film showing her *Dying Swan* (see *DM*, January 1976); for proper effect this solo should be projected at "silent speed" (18 frames per second) with the sound left on. See also IMMORTAL SWAN.

BALLET FOR ALL—6: BALLET COMES TO BRITAIN. 26 min., 1970, b/w.*

*Rental $13 from Illinois. Sale $340 from Heritage.*
Mostly on Diaghilev, despite the title. Three portions of the Ballet Rambert version of Nijinsky's *Afternoon of a Faun* are danced by Christopher Bruce and Marilyn Williams: the opening, the "courting" duet for the faun and the tall nymph, and the last portion. Then the cancan duet from Massine's *Boutique Fantasque* (1919) is danced by Brenda Last and Johaar Mosaval, and the hostess' solo from Nijinska's *Les Biches* (1924) is beautifully performed by Deanne Bergsma (to the accompaniment of much chatter from Blair). Diaghilev's contribution is assessed, George Balanchine gets his only mention in the series, and the program concludes with nine minutes of excerpts from de Valois' *The Rake's Progress* (1935) with a fine cast led by David Wall

and Alfreda Thorogood. (During the madhouse scene Blair informs us that this ballet is "English through and through.")

A comparison of the excerpts from *Afternoon of a Faun* with the stills of Nijinsky incorporated into the film AFTERNOON OF A FAUN suggests that the Rambert version is rather wide of the mark.

BALLET FOR ALL—7: BRITISH BALLET TODAY. 29 min., 1970, b/w.**

*Rental $14 from Illinois. Sale $340 from Heritage.*
Three-quarters of this program, probably the best in the series, is devoted to portions of Frederick Ashton's delightful *La Fille Mal Gardée* (1960).

David Blair turns over the microphone to Peter Brinson (who proves to be a superior narrator) in order to recreate his original role of Colas to Brenda Last's Lise and Ronald Emblem's Widow Simone. Emphasizing how Ashton (like de Valois) is able to blend character with dancing, the excerpts, linked by narration, include the ribbon solos for Lise and Colas, their flirtatious duet, the Widow's warmly daffy clog dance, and the tender and exquisite final wedding duet. Also shown is the beautiful mime scene in which Lise blissfully and innocently imagines her married life with Colas. (This scene, presumably created by Ivanov in 1885, was remembered and relayed to Ashton by Tamara Karsavina; she writes of it in Ivor Guest's *La Fille Mal Gardée*: "The visions of future felicity, of her children to come is a blend of budding maternal love and of a girl playing with her dolls.")

The film opens with a portion of the pleasant duet from Kenneth MacMillan's *Concerto* danced by Patricia Ruanne and Kerrison Cooke.

BALLET GIRL. 23 min., b/w.

*Rental $8.50 from Syracuse, $15 from Audio Brandon. Sale $160 from Audio Brandon.*
Fictionalized documentary of a young student in the school of the Royal Danish Ballet. Contains virtually no stage dancing, although film listings sometimes suggest otherwise.

BALLET IN JAZZ. 11 min.

*Rental $12.50 from Audio Brandon.*
A German ballet approach to jazz and jazz dance.

BALLET OF THE PARIS OPERA. 9 min., 1930s, b/w.

*Rental $4 from Kentucky.*
Views of the Paris Opéra house, audience, and backstage. Excerpt from *Suite de Danse* is performed.

## BALLET OF THE 20TH CENTURY—AMERICAN DEBUT. 20 min., color.*

*Rental free from Films and Broadcasting, International Telephone and Telegraph, 320 Park Avenue, NYC 10022.*

The first performance in the United States of Maurice Béjart's Belgian company at the Brooklyn Academy of Music in January 1971. Includes excerpts from three works: *Choreographic Offering* and *Bhakti* (with Paolo Bortoluzzi) and *Erotica* (with Suzanne Farrell and Daniel Lommel). For a review, see Marcia B. Siegel, *At the Vanishing Point*, pp. 127-128, et seq.

## BALLET WITH EDWARD VILLELLA. 27 min., 1970, color.*

*Rental $10.50 from Kent State, $12 from Kentucky, $12.20 from Michigan, $12.40 from Minnesota, $12.50 from Boston, $13.23 from South Florida, $13.50 from Illinois, $13.50 from Southern Illinois, $14 from Indiana, $15 from Penn State, $18 from Syracuse, $20 from USC, $30 from LCA. Sale $380 from LCA.*

Villella, with Patricia McBride and other members of the New York City Ballet, suggests through talk and demonstration what he feels ballet is all about. An able presentation, on the whole attractively photographed.

The dance episodes, all in full costume, include the male variation, the female variation, and the adagio (in that order, with talk in between) from George Balanchine's *Tchaikovsky Pas de Deux*. (The coda from this work, danced by Melissa Hayden and Jacques d'Amboise is included in the film, DANCE: NEW YORK CITY BALLET.) In addition, Villella mimes his way through Albrecht's entrance from Act II of *Giselle* and offers a fine performance of the solo preceding the duet with Terpsichore from Balanchine's *Apollo*. Finally, there are excerpts from the last movement of Balanchine's *Rubies*—the first third of the movement and the last third—in which Villella and McBride are joined by Marnee Morris and the corps.

The music for the *Rubies* segment seems out of sync with the picture, undercutting much of the impact of Balanchine's marvelously witty choreography, although the flavor of the piece does still come across. The camera work is also overly busy on the *Rubies* portion, but it is fine on the other dance exceprts. Produced by Robert Saudek.

## BALLET'S GOLDEN AGE. 10 min., 1957, color.

*Rental $5 from Syracuse, $5.20 from Minnesota, $5.50 from Kent State, $5.75 from Illinois, $8 from UCLA.*

Commentary, showing contemporary prints of the Romantic period, 1830-1846. Of very limited value.

## BASHFUL BALLERINA. 19 min., 1937, b/w.

*Rental $6.50 from Em Gee, $7.50 from Kit Parker.*
Nutty short featuring Imogene Coca.

## BAYADERKA. 10 min. 1943, b/w.*

*Rental $4 ($8 in the East) from Utah, $5 from Indiana, $5 from Syracuse, $8.50 from Audio Brandon. Sale $85 from Audio Brandon.*

Moments from the Shades scene (Act IV). Petipa's choreography had been revised by Chabukiani for a new Kirov version in 1941. He dances this pyrotechnic excerpt with Dudinskaya and corps. Also on BALLET CONCERT. For discussion of the choreography, see *Dance and Dancers*, October 1971, and George Balanchine's comments in his *New Complete Stories of the Great Ballets*.

## BEAUTY AND THE BEAST BALLET. 50 min., color.

*Rental $19 from South Florida, $50 from Audio Brandon, $50 from Association. Sale $605 from Audio Brandon.*

The San Francisco Ballet in a work by Lew Christensen.

## BEAUTY KNOWS NO PAIN. 25 min., 1973, color.*

*Rental $13 from Illinois, $13.50 from Indiana, $20 from Syracuse, $26 from California.*

Devastating documentary on the initiation and training of the nationally known football half-time drill team, the Rangerettes.

## BEHIND THE SCENES WITH THE ROYAL BALLET. 30 min., 1965, b/w.*

*Rental $9 from Syracuse, $15 from Budget.*

Contains rehearsal sequences from Kenneth MacMillan's *Romeo and Juliet* with Rudolf Nureyev partnering Margot Fonteyn and with Christopher Gable partnering Lynn Seymour. There is also a sequence showing Frederick Ashton rehearsing or choreographing Anthony Dowell, Vyvyan Lorrayne, and Robert Mead (the original cast) in a movement from *Monotones II* to one of the Erik Satie *Gymnopédies*. The same dancers perform this movement in full costume in the film, OPUS.

## BEJART. 18 min., 1961, b/w.

*Rental $20, sale $150, probably, from Radim.*
Shows Maurice Béjart in a teaching session with three other dancers, Tania Bari, Marie-Claire Carrie,

and Germinal Casado. They practice expressing in dance what they feel about different aural or visual stimuli: a verse, Japanese calligraphy, a modern painting. Commentary by Béjart is translated in English subtitles.

## BEJART FILMS.

*Several films on and by the Maurice Béjart Company rent free (but sometimes with difficulty) from Belgian Consulate General, 100 Bush Street, San Francisco, CA 94104; (415) 986-2883.*

## THE BIX PIECES. 30 min., 1973, color, videotape.?**

*For purchase on videotape only. See CAMERA THREE. May have been withdrawn.*

A program from CBS' *Camera Three* series showing a performance of Twyla Tharp's 1971 dance work.

The work is a set of dances combined with a kind of lecture-demonstration, offhandedly serious and movingly personal, in which Tharp discusses the construction of the dance, its relation to the music, and her notions about the interrelationships among dance styles. It is set to music by Bix Beiderbecke as well as Joseph Haydn and Thelonius Monk. The dancers are Tharp, Rose-Marie Wright, Kenneth Rinker, Sara Rudner, and Isabel Garcia-Lorca, while Tharp's text is declaimed by actress Marion Hailey. Ably directed by Merrill Brockway.

## BLACK TIGHTS. 120 min., 1962, color.

*Rental $40 from ROA.*

Four films with choreography by Roland Petit: THE DIAMOND CRUNCHER, CYRANO, A MERRY MOURNING, and CARMEN. Dancers include Renée ("Zizi") Jeanmaire, Moira Shearer, Cyd Charisse, Hans Van Manen, Henning Kronstam, and Petit.

## BLUE STUDIO. 10 min., 1977, color, videotape.*

*Rental and sale (on videotape only) from Cunningham Dance Foundation.*

A nicely crafted solo for video, choreographed and danced by Merce Cunningham. Direction by Charles Atlas.

## THE BODY AS AN INSTRUMENT (Murray Louis). See DANCE AS AN ART FORM.

## BOLERO. 15 min., 1960s, b/w.*

*Rental $13 from Rochester. Also sometimes available free from Cultural Services, Belgian Embassy, 3330 Garfield Street N.W., Washington, D. C. 20008. Sale from Productions Pierre Levie, 44 Vieille Halle aux Blés, Brussels 1000, Belgium.*

A good film of Maurice Béjart's highly theatrical ballet (for one woman on a large table top surrounded by forty men) to the equally theatrical Ravel score. Danced by Béjart's Ballet of the 20th Century and directed by Jean-Marc Landier.

As a possible companion, there is an interesting film on the music featuring a performance by Zubin Mehta and the Los Angeles Philharmonic. This film, also called BOLERO (28 min., 1972, color), can be rented for $10.50 from Kent State, $13 from Minnesota, $13 from Indiana, $13.50 from Illinois.

BOLERO

## THE BOLSHOI BALLET. 99 min., 1956, color.? **

*Probably available for rental on 35mm, unclear about 16mm rentals. Contact Mr. Robert Stracher, Pergamon Press, 395 Sawmill Road, Elmsford, NY 10523; (914) 592-7700. Possibly available for rental in 16mm, with advance planning, from Connoisseur Films Limited, 167 Oxford Street, London, W1R 2DX, England.*

An excellent film, produced by Paul Czinner and featuring Galina Ulanova in her most famous role: *Giselle*. The ballet is largely complete; missing are the *Peasant Pas de Deux* from Act I and opening portions of Act II including Giselle's initiation and the "first" duet with Albrecht (danced by Nikolai Fadeyechev). Rimma Karelskaya dances Myrtha.

Also on the film are *Dance of the Tartars*, "Spanish Dance" from *Swan Lake*, Asaf Messerer's *Spring Water* (with Lyudmila Bogomolova and Stanislav Vlasov), a *Dying Swan* by Ulanova, and dance excerpts from the operas *Faust* and *Ivan Susanin*.

## THE BOLSHOI BALLET TOURS AMERICA. 45 min., 1959, b/w. ?

*Possibly available for rental from NCA-SF.*

A documentary on the Bolshoi's 1959 tour, the film mostly shows the dancers as tourists: ogling at

Wall Street, chuckling at modern art, frolicking at Disneyland, and visiting with Bette Davis, Van Cliburn, Albert Kahn, William Randolph Hearst, Jr. Along the way, dance excerpts are shown, the longest being scenes of Ulanova in *Romeo and Juliet* and performing half of a *Dying Swan* (very unlike her filmed version from earlier years which can be seen on BALLET CONCERT). There are also bits from *Giselle* Act II, *Swan Lake*, *Flames of Paris*, *Stone Flower*, and *Chopiniana* featuring Plisetskaya, Ekaterina Maximova, Fadeyechev, and others.

Easily the most remarkable sequence, however, occurs in the visit to the New York City Ballet. The Bolshoi dancers are shown uncomprehendingly watching a segment from George Balanchine's *Agon*. Afterwards, the two companies greet each other at an animated reception, and Soviet choreographer Leonid Lavrovsky is shown talking to Balanchine, telling him, according to the narrator, "This sort of art has no future." The whole bizarre episode is discussed in Bernard Taper's *Balanchine*, pp. 281-288.

## BRANDENBURG CONCERTO NO. 4. 11 min., 1963, b/w.

*Rental $5 from Illinois, $5 from USC, $6 from Ohio State. Sale $60 from Ohio State, $70 from USC.*

A rather poor performance, by Ohio State students, of Doris Humphrey's last work, directed by Ruth Currier. Includes only the first movement.

## CAMERA THREE. A series of 30 min. videotapes.**

*Many of these fine CBS half-hour programs are available to educational institutions on videotape from PACT, Media Duplication and Distribution Service, N. Y. State Education Dept., Bureau of Mass Communications, Albany, NY 12224; (518) 474-2241. They dub the programs on videotapes sent to them. The service is free to institutions in New York state and costs $37.50 per program for those elsewhere. The programs are not available on film.*

Twyla Tharp's THE BIX PIECES and a two-part VIDEO EVENT by Merce Cunningham are described in separate listings. Among other dance programs one can get are: "Dances of Youth and Maturity" (Lone Isaksen and Lawrence Rhodes dance John Butler and Richard Wagner), "Coach with Six Insides" (Jean Erdman), "Over the Top Bebop" (jazz dancing), "Poem" (Sophie Maslow), "As I Lay Dying" (Valerie Bettis), "Jan's Pantomime" (Jan Kessler), "Dances of India" (Nala Najan), "Moving Together: Mind and Body," "Today's Dancer" (Walter Terry), "Ballet Episodes" (Terry/James Clauser), "Illuminations," "Matteo and the Indo-American Dance Company," four programs on Béjart, and programs on the dance of Morocco, Cambodia, Iran, Sierra Leone, Bali, and Pakistan.

## CANADA AT 8:30. 28 min., color.

This is not a dance film, although it frequently appears in catalogs under the dance heading. A documentary on performing arts in Canada (presented by Volkswagen), there is one fleeting glimpse of Brian MacDonald and the Royal Winnipeg Ballet.

## CARNIVAL OF RHYTHM. 20 min., 1941, color.

*Rental (members only) $20, sale $200 from Dance Films.*

Katherine Dunham and company in South American and African dances.

## CAROUSEL. 128 min., 1956, color. Also available in cinemascope.*

*Rental $40 from Films Inc.*

Dance usually gets undercut when a Broadway show is subjected to Hollywood treatment. In this case, however, Agnes de Mille's original Broadway dream dance, "Louise's Ballet," seems to have been faithfully retained by the film's choreographer, Rod Alexander. It features a lovely adagio (for Jacques d'Amboise and Susan Luckey) and an ingenious fantasy-carousel formed by a ring of posturing dancers. Also included is a boisterous romp to "June is Bustin' Out All Over," choreographed by Alexander.

## CHERRY TREE CAROL. See AGNES DE MILLE'S A CHERRY TREE CAROL.

## CHILDREN OF THEATRE STREET. 90 min., 1977, color.

*Information from Mack-Vaganova Co., 415 E. 52 Street, NYC 10022; (212) 755-2518.*

Documentary on the Kirov School in Leningrad.

## A CHOREOGRAPHER AT WORK. 29 min., 1960, b/w.

*Rental $7.50 ($15 in East) from Utah, $7.70 from Iowa, $9.50 from Indiana, $11 from Association. Sale $125 from Indiana.*

A discussion with John Butler about the creation of a dance work. With Bambi Linn and his company, Butler performs several excerpts from his works and the complete *Three Promenades to the Lord*. Part of Martha Myers' "A Time to Dance" series.

## CHOREOGRAPHY. 11 min., 1960, b/w.

*Rental $12.50 from Audio Brandon.*

A German film about the creation of a ballet, with Heinz Claus.

CHRONIQUES DE FRANCE. A series of 25 min., b/w films.

*Information from FACSEA.*
Each film covers three or four aspects of life in France. Among the dance subjects touched upon are: *Les Ballets Blaska, A Ballet by Darius Milhaud, Maurice Béjart, Michel Denard, The Contemporary Ballet Theatre.*

CHRYSALLIS. 22 min., 1973, color.*

*Rental $24 from FMC.*
A half-serious, half-playful film by Ed Emshwiller featuring the Alwin Nikolais Company.

CINDERELLA. 80 min., 1961, color.

*Rental $125 ($75 classroom) from Willoughby/ Peerless, 115 W. 31 Street, NYC 10001. May also be available from Art Cinema Booking Service, 1501 Broadway, NYC 10036.*
Zakharov's choreography danced by Raisa Struchkova and the Bolshoi Ballet. A new dimension in garishness.

CIRCLES II. 8 min., 1974, color.*

*Rental $5.50 from Kent State, $6 from Indiana, $12 from Syracuse, $12 from Viewfinders.*
Imaginative cine-dance film by Doris Chase. See also DORIS CHASE.

CLAIRE DE LUNE. 5 min., color.

*Rental $5 from Minnesota.*
Ballerina Diana Budaska dances against the background of a formal garden on the Canary Islands.

CLASSICAL BALLET. 29 min., 1960, b/w.*

*Rental $9.50 from Indiana, $11 from UCLA, $11 from Association. Sale $125 from Indiana.*
A discussion of the history of ballet with demonstrations of steps by Marina Eglevsky and others and with a performance of the coda to Petipa's *Bluebird Pas de Deux* by Linda Yourth and George Li. Maria Tallchief and Andre Eglevsky join the discussion and perform the coda to the *Sylvia Pas de Deux* (choreography presumably by Balanchine) and (without corps) the Act II adagio from *Swan Lake*. Part of Martha Myers' "A Time to Dance" series.

COLLEGE KALEIDESCOPE. 29 min., color.

*Rental $6 from South Florida.*
Blending of dance, music, and film effects. In-cludes the dance group from the University of South Florida directed by William Hug.

CONCERT OF STARS. 86 min., 1952, b/w.

*Rental $50 (higher for large audiences or where admission is charged) from Audio Brandon.*
Includes Galina Ulanova and Vladimir Preobrazhenski in the waltz pas de deux from *Les Sylphides* (also available separately—see LES SYLPHIDES); Natalia Dudinskaya and Konstantine Sergeyev in scenes from *Raymonda*; scenes, including the sabre dance, from *Gayne*; and the Moiseyev Dance Company in *The Strollers* (also available separately—see MOISEYEV DANCERS). There are also scenes (with subtitles) from operas (Tchaikovsky's *Queen of Spades*, Glinka's *Ivan Susanin*) and from Shostakovich's oratorio, *Song of the Forests*.

CONTEMPORARY DANCE SERIES. 1970, b/w. ?

*Rental probably from Michigan.*
Eight films on modern dance and education.

CONTINUUM. 20 min., 1965, b/w.

*Rental $7.50 ($15 in East) from Utah.*
Master's thesis film by Susan Wheeler.

CONVERSATION IN THE ARTS: DANCE. 21 min., color.

*Rental probably from Audio-Visual Utilization Center, Wayne State University, Detroit, MI 48202; (313) 577-2424.*
Agnes de Mille is interviewed.

COPPELIA. 8 min., b/w. X

Divertissements from Act III with Myrna Galle and Fernand Nault. Filmed outdoors at the Cloisters in New York. Clumsy. Apparently no longer available.

CORTEGE OF EAGLES. 38 min., 1969, color.**

*Rental $12.90 from Illinois, $13 from Minnesota, $16 from Penn State, $20 from Budget, $25 from Pyramid. Sale $375 from Pyramid.*
Martha Graham's version of Queen Hecuba's trials during the Trojan War, choreographed in 1967.
The work begins with visions of Hecuba and of the impassive Helen, who brought the war to Troy by deserting the Greeks (and her Greek husband) in favor of Paris, one of Hecuba's sons. Chorus passages suggest the themes of war and of maternity. Charon, as a kind of supernatural stage manager, leads the characters in a briefly suggested dumb show of the tragedy to come. He claps his hands and the drama begins with a pre-war scene of domestic contentment in Troy: King Priam presents a gift to Hecuba, while

Hector, their son, dances a love duet with his wife, Andromache. The war comes to Troy with the arrival of the Greek hero, Achilles, who challenges Hector and makes advances to Hecuba's daughter, Polyxena. Hector is killed in the battle with Achilles, and Polyxena kills herself rather than submit to the victor. The chorus wails and laments.

Hecuba then sends her youngest son with gold for safekeeping to the King of Thrace who kills the boy and steals the treasure. Helen walks by, unconcerned. Hector's young son is dragged from the arms of his mother to be sacrificed to the God of War. The King of Thrace now visits Hecuba and feigns friendship, but she has learned of her youngest son's murder at his hands and tempts the King into her ruined city. There, she now resorts to the violence that has surrounded her, blinding the murderer, and is seen as the work ends pathetically caressing the blinding weapon with maternal tenderness.

The work is based mostly on two plays by Euripides: *The Trojan Women* and *Hecuba*. The music is by Eugene Lester, the settings by Isamu Noguchi. Adapted for the camera by John Butler. Directed by Dave Wilson. The color is somewhat faded in quality. The cast:

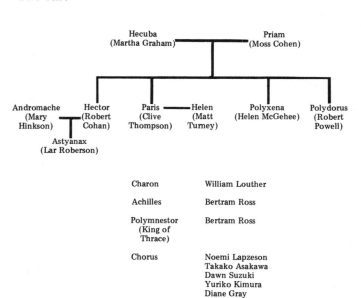

| Charon | William Louther |
| Achilles | Bertram Ross |
| Polymnestor (King of Thrace) | Bertram Ross |
| Chorus | Noemi Lapzeson<br>Takako Asakawa<br>Dawn Suzuki<br>Yuriko Kimura<br>Diane Gray |
| The Warriors | Clive Thompson<br>Moss Cohen<br>Robert Dodson<br>Kenneth Pearl<br>Hugh Appet |

A feature film of Euripides play, THE TROJAN WOMEN, can be rented from Swank for $150. It features Katharine Hepburn, Vanessa Redgrave, Geneviève Bujold, and Irene Papas and is directed by Michael Cacoyannis.

CUBA—ART AND REVOLUTION. 46 min., 1971, color.

*Rental $18.25 from Iowa, $18.25 from Indiana, $18.80 from Michigan, $55 from Time-Life. Sale $550 from Time-Life.*

BBC-TV documentary that includes a visit with ballerina Alicia Alonso. See also ALICIA.

THE DANCE. 74 min., b/w.

*Rental $40 (higher for large audiences or where admission is charged) from Audio Brandon.*

An unsatisfactory German-made survey. Millions of snippets.

DANCE: ANNA SOKOLOW'S ROOMS. 30 min., 1966, b/w.**

*Rental $6 from Minnesota, $6.60 from Northern Illinois, $9.50 from Indiana, $10.50 from UCLA, $11 from Penn State, $13 from California.*

The important 1955 study of loneliness and isolation in the jazz age is performed by a group including Ze'eva Cohen, Jack Moore, and Jeff Duncan. Three sections of the work are not included on the film: a male solo called "Dream," a short female solo called "The End," and a trio called "Daydream."

The 1950s jazz score is by Kenyon Hopkins. Also appearing are Margaret Cicierska, Martha Clarke, Kathryn Posin, Ray Cook, and Chester Wolenski. Directed by Dave Geisel. Part of the "USA: Dance" series.

DANCE—A REFLECTION OF OUR TIMES. 29 min., 1960, b/w.*

*Rental $7.80 from Boston, $9.50 from Indiana, $11 from Association. Sale $125 from Indiana.*

A discussion with Herbert Ross about the use of dance as social commentary and the relation of dance to other art forms. Ruth Ann Koesun and John Kriza perform a fine duet from Ross' *Paeon* based on a love poem of Sappho and then are joined in a complete performance of Ross' powerful *Caprichos* (1949) by Jennie Workman, Sallie Wilson, Lupe Serrano, Scott Douglas, Enrique Martinez, and Emy St. Just. Ross tells about the creation of *Caprichos* and shows the savage Goya etchings on which it is based. Part of Martha Myers' "A Time to Dance" series. For a suggestion on presentation, see p. 13.

DANCE AS AN ART FORM. A series of five films in color, produced between 1972 and 1974, each running between 26 and 32 min.*

*Each rents for $50, sells for $500, from Chimera-film, 33 E. 18 Street, NYC 10003; (212) 777-1120. The set of five can be rented for $200, purchased for $2000. (Those in Indiana or Connecticut—see p. 3.)*

The films are perky and engaging, if somewhat redundant and quite overpriced. Directed and master-minded by Murray Louis, they are called, in some sort of order, THE BODY AS AN INSTRUMENT, MOTION, SPACE, TIME, and SHAPE. As a sample, MOTION is suggested because it seems to have the most kinetic appeal. A close second would be THE BODY AS AN INSTRUMENT.

Each film is a sequential collage of movement ideas, shot both in the studio and outdoors at various scenic locations. Featured are Louis and his dance company, sundry collections of college students, children, and an occasional animal. There is a narration written and performed by Louis that attempts to relate the visual material to the concept under consideration in the individual film, but the dismemberment of the choreographer's medium is not entirely successful. Any dancing body will illustrate motion, form a shape, and take up space and time, so the pattern taken for illustration of the concept will be ambiguous and, with a few exceptions, could be used in any of the films.

However, the films are quite beautifully photographed (the camera work is by Warren Lieb) and, for the most part, well-paced, applying an appealing, mildly zany sense of humor. The camera setups are simple and direct and are nicely composed, usually to allow the movement to be expressed by the bodies under view rather than by the camera.

Samples of Louis' quirky choreography are distributed throughout the films in two- or three-minute chunks, which will be good news to those who think his invention wears thin after about that long. Among these are excerpts from the *Personnae* quartet on BODY and MOTION; moments from *Proximities* (to Johannes Brahms) on SPACE; parts of Louis' solo *Chimera* on TIME and SHAPE; and a male duet from *Calligraph for Martyrs* and part of Louis' solo *Index (to necessary neuroses. . .)* on SHAPE. In addition, there is a performance of Alwin Nikolais' *Noumenon* featuring two seated men in all-encompassing sacks, at the end of SPACE. The dance excerpts are very effectively filmed, mostly in the studio using a single, fairly passive camera with dissolves to link takes.

The bulk of the footage was apparently shot without sound, and a score, consisting mostly of Alwin Nikolais' cheerful electronic pixilations, has been added. Other dancers on the films, besides Louis, include Michael Ballard, Caroline Carlson, Les Ditson, Helen Kent, Lynn Levine, Anne McLeod, Robert Small, Marcia Wardell, Gladys Bailin, Raymond Johnson, Richard Biles, Gerald Otte, Phyllis Lamhut,

Raymond Clay, and Claudia Melrose. For a view of Louis as a dancer in younger days, see INVENTION IN DANCE.

DANCE CHROMATIC. 7 min., 1959, color.

*Rental $10 from FMC.*
A film by Ed Emshwiller that fuses dance and abstract painting, to a score by Lou Harrison.

DANCE CLASS. 9 min., color.

*Rental $7.50 from Syracuse. Rental $10, sale $140 from Audio Brandon.*
The Toronto Dance Theatre seen in classes taught by Peter Randazzo as well as in rehearsal for a work called *A Thread of Sand*. From National Film Board of Canada.

DANCE: ECHOES OF JAZZ. 29 min., 1965, b/w.*

*Rental $6 from Minnesota, $6.60 from Northern Illinois, $7.80 from Boston, $9.50 from Indiana, $11 from Penn State.*
Three specially-commissioned dances by Donald McKayle, Grover Dale, and John Butler are used to trace jazz dance from the tap of the 1930s to the cool of the 1960s. Danced by Honi Coles, Paula Kelley, Dudley Williams, William Louther, John Butler, Mary Hinkson, Buzz Miller, Grover Dale, and Michel Harty. Part of the "USA: Dance" series.

DANCE FESTIVAL. 11 min., 1938, b/w.

*Rental $2 from Kentucky, $5 from Illinois, $5 from Syracuse, $6.75 from Indiana, $9 from Audio Brandon. Sale $85 from Audio Brandon.*
Dances of the Ukraine, Uzbekistan, Armenia, and the Caucasus by successful Soviet contestants at an International Dance Festival in London.

DANCE: FOUR PIONEERS. 29 min., 1965, b/w.**

*Rental $6 from Minnesota, $6.60 from Northern Illinois, $7.50 from UCLA, $7.50 ($15 in East) from Utah, $7.80 from Boston, $7.90 from Illinois, $9.50 from Indiana, $11 from Penn State, $13 from California, $16 from Rochester. Sale $165 from Indiana.*
The first half of this fine film is a documentary on modern dance in the 1930s, particularly the Bennington experience. Discusses the perspectives of Martha Graham, Hanya Holm, Doris Humphrey, and Charles Weidman and shows Barbara Morgan still photographs, film clips from Bennington, and a portion of the film of Humphrey's AIR FOR THE G STRING.

The second half is a complete performance of Humphrey's *Passacaglia*, staged by Lucy Venable and featuring Chester Wolenski and Lola Huth. Part of the "USA: Dance" series. Directed by Charles S. Dubin. Extensive analytic notes by John Mueller for this film may be obtained from American Dance Guild, 152 W. 42 Street, NYC 10036.

## DANCE IN AMERICA.**

A series of high quality on public television, begun in 1976, produced by Merrill Brockway. Executive producer: Jac Venza. At the time of publication two of these programs were available on 16mm color film. They are discussed under their titles: MARTHA GRAHAM DANCE COMPANY and SUE'S LEG: REMEMBERING THE THIRTIES. For information about other programs that might become available on film, contact Audrey Weiss, WNET, 356 W. 58 Street, NYC 10019.

## DANCE IN DARK AND LIGHT. 8 min., 1970, color. ?

*Rental $10, sale $60 probably from BFA.*
A study for camera and dancers' silhouettes.

## DANCE: IN SEARCH OF "LOVERS." 29 min., 1966, b/w.*

*Rental $6 from Minnesota, $7.90 from Illinois, $9.50 from Indiana, $11 from Penn State, $11 from Association, $13 from California. Sale $165 from Indiana.*
Documentary on the creation of Glen Tetley's dance work through months of effort to opening night. Carmen de Lavallade and Mary Hinkson are shown as performers and in their private lives. Scott Douglas also appears, as do set designer Willa Kim and concert manager Norman Singer. Part of the "USA: Dance" series.

## DANCE INSTRUMENT. Five films, each 16-19 min., 1975, b/w.

*Rental $9 each from Illinois. Rental $20 each, sale $190 each from Athletic Institute, 705 Merchandise Mart, Chicago, IL 60654 (also available in Super 8).*
The films are on dance instruction and feature Lynda Davis and Clay Taliaferro: THE DANCE IN-STRUMENT:ALIGNMENT, THE DANCE INSTRU-MENT:HOW TO MOVE BETTER, DANCE DESIGN: EXPLORATIONS IN MOVEMENT, DANCE DE-SIGN:SHAPING, and DANCE DESIGN: SPACE.

## DANCE IN THE SUN. 7 min., 1953, b/w. ?

*Rental, probably $12.50, from McGraw-Hill.*
Shirley Clark's experimental film featuring a solo by Daniel Nagrin.

## DANCE: NEW YORK CITY BALLET. 29 min., 1965, b/w.**

*Rental $6 from Minnesota, $6.60 from Northern Illinois, $7.90 from Illinois, $9.50 from Indiana, $11 from Penn State, $11 from Association, $13 from California.*
An excellent film featuring choreography by George Balanchine: Suzanne Farrell and Arthur Mitchell in the entrée and most of the adagio from the *Agon* pas de deux, Patricia McBride and Edward Villella in the complete *Tarantella*, Farrell and Jacques d'Amboise in the complete *Meditation*, and Melissa Hayden and d'Amboise in the coda from the *Tchaikovsky Pas de Deux*. (The rest of this last duet is on BALLET WITH EDWARD VILLELLA.) Balanchine discusses his philosophy briefly and is seen in rehearsal and watching playback. Directed by Charles S. Dubin. Part of the "USA: Dance" series.

George Balanchine

## DANCE OF ECSTASY. 12 min., color, widescreen (special anamorphic lens required for projector—see p. 6). Also available in 35mm and videocassette.

*Rental $50 from Twyman.*
Anne Lise Borre, Fleming Steen, and Ingrid Bucholtz of the Royal Danish Ballet in a nude ballet,

photographed on a black reflective floor, to music by Scriabin. Directed by Brandon Chase.

## THE DANCE ON FILM: 1894-1912, PART I, BALLET. 20 min., color.*

*Rental $45, sale $300 from Weber.*
Turn of the century dance footage, some hand-colored. Includes several sequences from films by George Meliés and Pathé Frère. The famous Italian ballerina, Pierina Legnani, the first to perform thirty-two fouettés on pointe and the first Odette-Odile, is seen briefly, though not doing fouettés.

## THE DANCE ON FILM: 1894-1912, PART II, THE ART DANCER. 15 min., b/w.*

*Rental $15 from UCLA, $35 from Weber. Sale $250 from Weber.*
Created in part from paper prints deposited for copyright purposes with the Library of Congress around the turn of the century. It includes varieties of music hall dance filmed by Thomas Edison and others.

There are dances by three imitators of Loie Fuller, by Karina, by Princess Rajah (who frolics for forty-five seconds with a kitchen chair clutched in her teeth), by Ella Lola, and, from about 1899, by someone who may be Isadora Duncan. Also included are sections of a feature film about a female Dracula. The added music is mostly inappropriate. (See Walter Terry's exuberant column, *Saturday Review*, March 8, 1969.) See also EARLY DANCE FILMS and HISTORICAL FILMS.

## DANCE: ROBERT JOFFREY BALLET. 30 min., 1965, b/w.**

*Rental $6 from Minnesota, $6.60 from Northern Illinois, $7.50 ($15 in East) from Utah, $7.80 from Boston, $9.50 from Indiana, $11 from Penn State, $11 from Association, $13 from California.*
A documentary on the company including brief excerpts from Joffrey's *Pas de Déesses* and *Gamelan*, and Anna Sokolow's *Opus 65*, a longer excerpt from Gerald Arpino's *Incubus* (featuring Lisa Bradley), and the second and fourth movements from Arpino's *Viva Vivaldi* (featuring Robert Blankshine and Luis Fuente). Part of the "USA: Dance" series.

## DANCE THEATRE OF ALWIN NIKOLAIS. 31 min., 1964, b/w. X

*Had been available from Illinois, but apparently is no more.*
Includes the dancers of the Henry Street Playhouse in Nikolais' *Reliquary*, *Carillon*, *Clown Dance*, *Duet*,

and *Celebrants*. Produced by WCBS-TV, New York, as part of their Repertoire Workshop series.

## DANCERS IN SCHOOL. 28 min., 1972, color.

*Rental $13.50 from Penn State, $15 from Pennebaker. Sale $250 from Pennebaker.*
A documentary on Murray Louis, Virginia Tanner, and Bella Lewitzky as dancers in residence teaching in the public schools.

## A DANCER'S GRAMMAR. 16 min., 1977, color.*

*Rental $28.50, sale $285 from Phoenix.*
A film by Nina Feinberg showing dancers Lois Bewley and Lawrence Rhodes in various barre and center exercises, some filmed in slow motion.

Lawrence Rhodes in A DANCER'S GRAMMAR

## A DANCER'S WORLD. 30 min., 1957, b/w.**

*Rental $5.35 from Minnesota, $7.10 from Northern Illinois, $7.50 from Michigan, $7.50 from South Florida, $7.50 ($15 in East) from Utah, $8.20 from Southern Illinois, $8.90 from Iowa, $9.90 from Illinois, $10 from Kent State, $11 from Penn State, $13 from Syracuse, $15 from Audio Brandon, $18 from California, $25 from Viewfinders, $25 from Phoenix. Sale $250 from Phoenix.*
One of the most beautiful dance films ever made. As she dresses for the role of Jocasta (in NIGHT JOURNEY), Martha Graham discusses the life, the art, and the craft of the dancer. Her dancers, in the studio, flow through dance patterns from the Graham vocabulary and repertory (including *Diversion of Angels*).

Appearing are Yuriko, Helen McGehee, Gene MacDonald, Ellen Siegel, Robert Cohan, Miriam Cole,

David Wood, Lillian Biersteker, Bertram Ross, Ethel Winter, and Mary Hinkson. Graham's text is reprinted in *Dance Observer*, January 1958. Directed by Peter Glushanok.

## DANCES BY SUZUSHI HANAYAGI. 18 min., 1963, color.

*Rental $9.40 from Illinois.*
Three Japanese dances: "Kurokami," "Without Color," and "Vignettes."

## THE DANCING PROPHET. 27 min., 1970, color.

*Rental $10.75 from Minnesota, $11.50 from Illinois, $15 from USC, $20 from Pyramid, $20 from Budget. Sale $300 from Pyramid.*
A documentary on Ruth St. Denis making some effective use of still photographs but otherwise really terrible. There are some clumsily staged dance "re-creations," an excruciating sequence showing St. Denis wheezing up a hill, and minimally helpful interviews with Alicia Markova, Jack Cole, Anton Dolin, and the dancer herself (with the camera far too close). All this in glaring color. Written and directed by Edmund Penney. Far to be preferred are the films RUTH ST. DENIS AND TED SHAWN, FIRST LADY OF THE AMERICAN DANCE, and RUTH ST. DENIS BY BARIBAULT.

## DAY ON EARTH. 21 min., 1978, color.**

*Rental $20, sale $285 from Rochester.*
A beautiful, simple record filming by Dwight Godwin of the 1947 Doris Humphrey masterpiece as performed in 1972 by Juilliard dancers Peter Sparling, Janet Eilber, Ann de Gange, and Elizabeth Haight.
In this moving work, the choreographer warmly portrays the life of a man as he relates to an early love, to his wife, to their child. There are life's trials and the anguish of leave-taking and death, but solace is found mostly through the medium of work. The music is Aaron Copland's *Piano Sonata*.

## DENISHAWN. 10 min., b/w.

*Rental $10 from Rochester.*
This historical film consists of two newsreel segments. The first was made in 1915 and shows scenes around the Denishawn School in Los Angeles. St. Denis and Ted Shawn are seen teaching class and administering the school, some of the students pose for the camera or frolic in the pool, and St. Denis shows off her peacock—a gift from Shawn. The second was made in 1930, with sound. In it St. Denis dances lively excerpts intended to demonstrate "the characteristic racial gestures" of dances from Siam, Java, and India (Nautch).

## THE DESPERATE HEART. 9 min., late 1940s, b/w.*

*Rental $3.50 from Boston, $3.70 from Michigan, $4.35 from Northern Illinois, $5 from Syracuse, $6.50 from Penn State, $10 from Audio Brandon. Sale $75 from Audio Brandon.*
Valerie Bettis' effective solo about melancholy and remembered happiness, choreographed in 1943 and filmed by Walter Strate. Bettis herself speaks the John Malcolm Brinnin poem that accompanies the dance. For a discussion of the work and the text of the poem, see Margaret Lloyd, *Borzoi Book of Modern Dance*, pp. 256-258.

## DR. COPPELIUS. 97 min., 1968, color.

*Rental $47.50 from Select; if not available from Select try AMS, 26 W. Merrick Road, P. O. Box 586, Valley Stream, NY 11582; (516) 599-1380.*
A version of the ballet *Coppélia* performed by the Gran Theatro del Liceo of Barcelona with Walter Slezak in the title role, Claudia Corday as Swanhilda, and Caj Selling as Franz. Alicia Markova is the artistic advisor. Directed by Ted Kneeland; produced by Frank J. Hale.

## DON QUIXOTE. 109 min., 1973, color. Also available in 35mm.**

*Rental probably from Illinois. Otherwise, available expensively from Paul Baise, Walter Reade, 241 E. 34 Street, NYC 10016; (212) 683-6300.*
Rudolf Nureyev and the Australian Ballet in a fine film of Nureyev's version of Marius Petipa's 1869 classic.
In general Nureyev seems to have kept most of the flavor and much of the choreography that was probably in the original version. The principal changes seem to be a sharpening of the plot line, a reduction of lengthy mime sequences, and an expansion of the lead made role danced, of course, by R. Nureyev.
The dancer's fans could not ask for much more. Nureyev is on the screen a great deal and is in fine form all the way through. If any of the takes showed him in an off moment, they have been judiciously left on the cutting-room floor by the director (R. Nureyev).
The camera work is generally quite effective. There is sometimes too much cutting to different angles and takes and sometimes too much reliance on shots from high angles, but the dancers are mostly kept fully in view and the choreography is treated sympathetically.
Cinematographer Geoffrey Unsworth's soft color is attractive, as are the sets and costumes of Barry Kay. The production was originally designed for the stage, however, and often the background clutter of people and properties is a bit too much for the camera eye. Bright projection is essential.

The Australian Ballet, led by Lucette Aldous and the sparkling Marilyn Rowe, is quite up to Nureyev's challenge, and the mysterious and austere Don Quixote of Robert Helpmann (who co-directed the film) is impressive.

DORIS CHASE.   Six films, 4-8 min. each, color.

*Rental $10 each, sale $100-$125 each from Audio Brandon.*

Six experimental multimedia dance films by Doris Chase:  DANCE FIVE (with Kei Takei), DANCE NINE (with Gus Solomons, Jr.), TALL ARCHES III (with Mary Staton Dance Ensemble), DANCE SEVEN (with Marnee Morris), DANCE ELEVEN (with Cynthia Anderson), and MOON GATES III (with Mary Staton Dance Ensemble).  For other films by Doris Chase, write FMC.  See also CIRCLES II.

DREAM OF AN ALCHEMIST.   12 min., color. ?

*Rental possibly $30 from Bouchard.*

Film by Thomas Bouchard based on a Hanya Holm/Kurt Seligmann work about alchemy.  Music composed for the film by Stanley Bate.  See also THE GOLDEN FLEECE.

DROTTNINGHOLM COURT THEATRE.   28 min., 1966, color.

*Rental $11.65 from Iowa.*

On the carefully preserved 200-year-old Swedish theater.

DYING SWAN.  3 min., 1973, b/w.

*Rental $8 from Rochester.*

In 1925, Fokine published a book describing exactly how he wanted this famous solo performed. The description included over fifty still photographs of his wife, Vera, in poses from the ballet, each numbered and precisely associated with the musical score.  This film displays these photographs in coordination with the Camille Saint-Saëns music and can be used to compare the choreographer's intentions with the several other versions available on film (see BALLET CONCERT, PLISETSKAYA DANCES, and TONIGHT WE SING for versions of Ulanova, Plisetskaya, and Toumanova, respectively).

It takes two or three viewings for the eye to see the motion through the flurry of stills but, once done, the musicality, dramatic approach, and technical difficulty of Fokine's version can be appreciated.

EARLY DANCE FILMS.  12 min., b/w, silent.*

*Rental $11 from Rochester.*

Eleven interesting and sometimes hilarious short dance films from 1894-1912 as restored from the Library of Congress paper print collection.

Included are: 1) "Crissie Sheridan," 2) "Ameta," and 3) "Annabella" (in color)—three imitators of Loie Fuller; 4) "Animated Picture Studio," a trick film which includes a flirtatious skirt dance done, perhaps, by Isadora Duncan (Walter Terry thinks that is who it is—see his exuberant column in *Saturday Review,* March 8, 1969); 5) "Flag Dance" showing one Annabelle Whitford Moore frolicking around while waving a small American flag; 6) "Turkish" and 7) "A La Trilby"—two provocative dances by variety dancer Ella Lola; 8) "French Acrobatic Dance" featuring a female trio; 9) "Little Lillian, Toe Danseuse" in some of the ugliest pointe work on record; 10) "Nymph of the Waves," a trick film featuring the Niagara Falls rapids, and the "Speedway Dance" of a real toe dancer, Catherina Bartho, who had studied with Enrico Cecchetti in Moscow and was featured at the Metropolitan Opera in the 1899-1900 season; and 11) "Princess Rajah" whose specialty was dancing with a kitchen chair clutched between her teeth.  See also DANCE ON FILM and HISTORICAL FILMS.

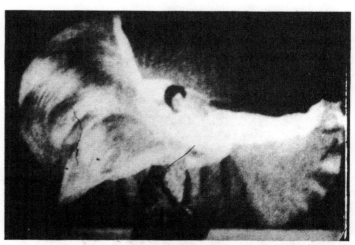

Ameta in EARLY DANCE FILMS

EMPEROR JONES. 26 min., 1978, color.*

*Rental $21, sale $300 from Rochester.  Also available from Illinois.*

José Limón's highly theatrical dance work based on the Eugene O'Neill play, choreographed in 1956. Filmed in 1972 in a somewhat underpowered performance by the professional Repertory Company of the American Dance Festival at Connecticut College, featuring Clay Taliaferro as Emperor Jones and Edward DeSoto as the White Man.  A record (fixed camera) film of the work is also available from Rochester. (A 1933 feature film of the play, with Paul Robeson in the title role, can be rented for $35 from Kit Parker, for $35 from Budget, or for $45 from Em Gee.)

## ENIGMA VARIATIONS. 33 min., 1970, color.**

*Rental $27 from Rochester.*

Both the choreography and atmosphere of the fine Frederick Ashton ballet of 1968 are preserved in this excellent film.

The original Royal Ballet cast dances, featuring Derek Rencher as Elgar, Svetlana Beriosova as Lady Elgar, Ann Jenner as Dorabella, and Desmond Doyle as Jaeger. Other solos are performed by Stanley Holden, Brian Shaw, Alexander Grant, Robert Mead, Vyvyan Lorrayne, Anthony Dowell, Georgina Parkinson, Wayne Sleep, Leslie Edwards, and Deanne Bergsma.

For a superb critical examination of this ballet, together with Ashton's program notes for the work, see *Dance and Dancers*, December 1968; for a discussion of the film and of the process of making it, see *Dance and Dancers*, September 1969. Directed by James Archibald.

## ENTR'ACTE. 18 min., 1924, b/w, silent.*

*Rental $7.50 from Kit Parker, $8 from Em Gee, $8 from Budget, $10 from Rochester, $16 from South Florida, $25 from MOMA. Sale $87.50 from EmGee.*

The chess game in ENTR'ACTE

René Clair's classic, zany, Dada-inspired, avant-garde film. Used as the middle section of the ballet *Relâche*, performed in December 1924 by the Swedish Ballet of Rolf de Maré. Scenario and design by Francis Picabia, music by Erik Satie, choreography by

Jean Borlin—all of whom appear on the film as do artists Marcel Duchamp and Man Ray (playing chess).

Relates in some ways to Merce Cunningham's WALKAROUND TIME. For an extended discussion, see *DM*, July 1977.

## ERICK HAWKINS 1964. 15 min., 1964, b/w.

*Rental $8, sale $90 from UCLA.*

The choreographer talks about his art and demonstrates.

## ERIK BRUHN—ARTIST OF THE BALLET. 21 min., 1971, color.

*Rental free from Danish Information Office, 280 Park Avenue, NYC 10017 and from Danish Consulate General, 3440 Wilshire Boulevard, Los Angeles, CA 90010.*

A portrait of the famous dancer in Copenhagen, Stockholm, and New York. Contains few dancing scenes.

## ETERNAL CIRCLE. 12 min., 1952, b/w.**

*Rental $8 from Rochester.*

Harald Kreutzberg in a solo work in which he plays multiple roles.

There are five rather grimly pathetic characters, each destined to strut and fret briefly until inevitably succumbing to the sardonic figure of Death: a bleary reveller or drunkard who is joined in a last, fatal drink by Death; a vain woman who sees the lurking figure in her mirror as she preens; a criminal who frees himself from a handcuffing rope only to be strangled by it; a wench or prostitute whose addled street dance is mocked by Death; and an aged king whose power topples with his crown and who watches mesmerized as his staff becomes a pendulum ticking away his last, impotent moments. The characters are differentiated by the choreography, by costumes, and, except for the figure of Death, by grotesque, stylized masks.

The work was originally done on the stage, choreographed in the late 1930s. On film it is possible, of course, to deal with the multiple role characterizations with considerable ease. But what is remarkable is how the dramatic and choreographic point of the dance work is carefully maintained and enhanced in the film version. Director Herbert Seggelke and Kreutzberg apply special film techniques, but these are used with such restraint and cunning that one scarcely notices. The film should furnish an object lesson to all gimmick-prone makers of dance films.

One of the most impressive of these effects occurs in the opening dance of Death. Kreutzberg was filmed crouched on the ground with his massive black cape spread out around him. From this position he rose, swirling, to full height. The film uses this footage in reverse so that the figure of Death seems to sink menacingly into the ground as his cloak oozes in an unnatural manner out from around him.

Another extraordinary moment occurs in the final, fatal section of the wench's dance. The passage is in stop-and-start slow motion so that she meets her doom by falling gradually to the ground in a rapid series of helpless and incoherent jerks.

The highly supportive music for the work is by Friedrich Wilckens, Kreutzberg's accompanist. See also PARACELSUS.

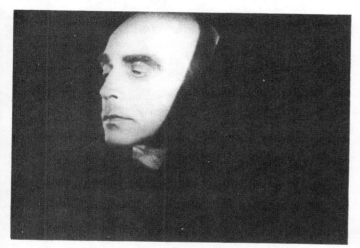

Harald Kreutzberg as Death in ETERNAL CIRCLE

ETHNIC DANCE: ROUNDTRIP TO TRINIDAD. 29 min., 1960, b/w.

*Rental $9.50 from Indiana, $11 from Association. Sale $125 from Indiana.*

A discussion with Geoffrey Holder and Carmen de Lavallade about the significance of ethnic dance in the field of formal dance. They perform West Indian dances including Bele (an adaptation of the minuet), Yanvollon (voodoo), and Banda (a Haitian dance about death). Part of Martha Myers' "A Time to Dance" series.

L'ETRANGER. 13 min., 1957, color.

*Rental $12 from FACSEA.*

Filmed ballet interpreted by Tania Bari, Antonio Carro, and the Maurice Béjart Ballet with music by Heitor Villa-Lobos. Narrates the tragic love story of a woman.

AN EVENING WITH THE ROYAL BALLET. 85 min., 1963, color.**

*Rental $125 (higher for large audiences or where admission is charged) from Audio Brandon or from*

*Association. Parts 1 and 2 can be rented separately for $25 each from Illinois. Sale from Audio Brandon.*

Four ballets filmed on the Royal Opera House stage at Covent Garden.

Part 1 begins with the company swirling its way through Frederick Ashton's rather dreary *La Valse*, a ballet one might consider not showing at all. The reel concludes with a beautiful rendering of Michel Fokine's complete *Les Sylphides* featuring Margot Fonteyn and the young Rudolf Nureyev, nicely filmed by Anthony Asquith. Fonteyn does an exquisite Prelude, Merle Park is seen in the Waltz, and Annette Page in the Mazurka. Nureyev's solo is done to a mazurka different from the one usually used in the West.

Part 2 begins with Nureyev dancing his version of the *Corsaire Pas de Deux* with Fonteyn. Both performers are in peak form—quite a peak—and, except for some mildly tacky camera work, the film works beautifully. Fonteyn is deliciously desirable, and Nureyev, just about definitive in this pantherine role, is ardent and desiring. The filmed duet is likely to be most effective if the sound is played loudly (but not distorted, of course). Nureyev seems to jump higher that way.

*La Valse* from EVENING WITH THE ROYAL BALLET

Part 2 concludes with roughly thirty minutes of *Aurora's Wedding* presented in the Royal Ballet's famous post-war version. Fonteyn, in probably her greatest role as the Princess, is splendid of course. She is paired with David Blair, who gives us a preposterously unprincely look-ma-no-hands grin at the end of the adagio, but generally looks princely enough. Brian Shaw is a good Bluebird, and his partner, Antoinette Sibley, is simply stunning. Brilliant solos (they may be cut on prints ordered from Audio Brandon outlets other than the Mt. Vernon home office) are also reeled off by Park and Georgina Parkinson, and the company as a whole does its posturing and polonaising and its fairytale stunts with ease and panache. The film is marred only slightly by the silly idea of director Asquith (or somebody) to have the bad fairy, Carabosse, make a fleeting appearance near the end of the act, ineffectually trying to menace the wedding celebrants.


FALL RIVER LEGEND. 10 min., 1972, color.

*Rental $5.50 from Kent State, $6 from Boston, $6.25 from Minnesota, $6.75 from Illinois, $8 from Syracuse. Sale $150 from ACI.*

Fragments from Agnes de Mille's ballet, based on the story of Lizzie Borden. Eccentrically filmed outdoors (at Sturbridge Village, Massachusetts), often with pointlessly severe camera angles.

Of little value except perhaps for the performances by members of American Ballet Theatre: Sallie Wilson, Gayle Young, Lucia Chase, and Tom Adair. Produced and directed by Bob Shanks.

FESTIVAL OF THE DANCE. 60 min., 1973, color.

*Rental $35, sale $590 from Rochester.*

A documentary on the creation of a special dance company to perform reconstructed modern dance classics (Humphrey, Graham, Weidman, Limón) at the 1972 American Dance Festival at Connecticut College. Filmed in the manner of PAUL TAYLOR AND COMPANY, but less lively and attractive. The dancers are seen winding up and winding down at auditions, rehearsals, performances, receptions, and meals.

The performance excerpts are brief and unsatisfying. Fortunately, full-length films of most of the reconstructed dance works were also made and this film is chiefly valuable in connection with them; see EMPEROR JONES, FLICKERS, NEW DANCE, VARIATIONS AND CONCLUSION FROM NEW DANCE, and WITH MY RED FIRES. The film, written and directed by Ted Steeg, also includes a brief overview of modern dance history.

FILM WITH THREE DANCERS. 20 min., 1970, color.

*Rental $20 from FMC.*

A film by Ed Emshwiller featuring members of the Alwin Nikolais company: Carolyn Carlson, Emery Hermans, and Bob Beswick.

THE FIRST LADY OF AMERICAN DANCE: RUTH ST. DENIS. 26 min., color.*

*Rental $50, probably from the producer, William Skipper, 65 South Lafayette, Mobile, AL 36604; or c/o Dance Films.*

St. Denis engagingly talks about, and then performs, four solos filmed late in her life: *White Jade, Black and Gold Sari, Cobra,* and *Yogi.*

FIRST POSITION. 90 min., 1972, color.*

*Rental from Arthur Cantor, Inc., 234 W. 44 Street, NYC 10036; (212) 391-0450.*

A fine fictionalized documentary on young dancers in the American Ballet Theatre School and their insecurities, poverty, ambitions.

Excerpts from *Petrouchka,* particularly from the second scene, are incorporated featuring Michael Smuin as Petrouchka. They are danced in costume in a ballet studio and apparently are intended to relate to the story of a potential love affair between a boy and a girl in the school. Extensive footage of rehearsals and classes featuring Yurek Lazowsky, Madame Valentina Pereyaslavec, and, especially, Leon Danielian. See *DM,* April 1972.

FLICKERS. 19 min., 1978, color.*

*Rental $20, sale $260 from Rochester. Also available from Illinois.*

Charles Weidman's zany spoof of silent movie conventions and clichés, choreographed in 1941. The film is of Weidman's 1972 reconstruction of the work for the professional Repertory Company at the American Dance Festival at Connecticut College. Linda Tarnay plays the Theda Bara-style seductress who also happens to be a leper, a role originally created, improbably, by Doris Humphrey. The work is in four "reels": "Hearts Aflame," "Wages of Sin," "Flowers of the Desert," and "Hearts Courageous."

FLUTE OF KRISHNA. 10 min., 1926, color, silent.

*Rental $8 from Rochester.*

A work composed by Martha Graham during the year she was with the Eastman School in Rochester, New York. Filmed by Eastman Kodak to experiment with a new two-color process, the work reflects Graham's Denishawn background in theme but seems, at the same time, to display a considerable original inventiveness and promise of things to come. Graham does not dance in the work herself. The unheard music was by Cyril Scott.

**498 THIRD AVENUE.** 120 min., 1968, b/w.?*

*Rental information from Cunningham Dance Foundation.*

An interesting documentary by Klaus Wildenham about the creation of Merce Cunningham's 1967 dance work *Scramble*. For a written description of the creation of this dance, see the chapter "An Appetite for Motion" in Calvin Tompkins, *The Bride and the Bachelors*.

**FUSION.** 15 min., 1967, color.**

*Rental free from Doris Thistlewood, Publicity Manager, Spring Mills, 104 W. 40 Street, NYC 10018, or for $8.50 from Illinois. Sale from Schoenfeld.*

A sprightly romp by filmmaker Ed Emshwiller and Alwin Nikolais making use of the Nikolais Company and of towels, sheets, and pillowcases by Spring Mills. See *Dance Perspectives* No. 30.

**GALINA ULANOVA.** 37 min., 1964, b/w.**

*Rental $10.90 from Illinois, $25 from USC, $30 from Audio Brandon. Sale $250 from Audio Brandon.*

An attractive documentary on the great ballerina showing clips from her life and from her many roles.

Includes nearly ten minutes from *Giselle* (with Konstantin Sergeyev): the wooing and mad scenes from Act I. There are also substantial moments from the *Swan Lake* Act II adagio, one of her versions of the *Dying Swan*, *Romeo and Juliet*, and the waltz pas de deux from *Les Sylphides*.

GALINA ULANOVA

**GAY PARISIAN (GAIETE PARISIENNE).** 20 min., 1941, color.*

*Rental $9 from Illinois, $17.50 from Em Gee, $20 (members only) from Dance Films. Sale from Dance Films.*

A shortened version of Leonide Massine's 1938 ballet in a Warner Brothers Production with dizzyingly busy camera direction by Jean Negulesco. Shows beautifully, however, a kind of character dancing difficult to find nowadays on the stage.

Features Massine as the Peruvian, Milada Mladova as the Glove Seller (replacing Alexandra Danilova who reportedly failed Hollywood's screen test), Frederic Franklin as the Baron, Nathalie Krassovska as the Flower Girl, with the Ballet Russe de Monte Carlo including Igor Youskevitch, Andre Eglevsky, Lubov Roudenko, Kazimir Kokich, and James Starbuck.

**GESTURES OF SAND.** 18 min., 1968, b/w.*

*Rental $8, sale $80 from UCLA.*

Explores the patterns of music, movement, ritual, and myth which were part of the life of the Jews of Aden, expressed through the unique artistry of Margalit Oved, formerly a leading dancer with the Inbal Dance Theater of Israel. Well photographed, well lighted. Directed by Allegra Fuller Snyder.

**GISELLE.** 56 min., 1950, b/w.

*Rental $37.50 from Em Gee.*

The stage is quite cramped, the sets and costumes a bit tacky, and the film quality murky in spots, but this film recording of a live NBC-TV production preserves the American Ballet Theatre performances of Nora Kaye as Giselle, Igor Youskevitch as Albrecht, and Diana Adams as Myrtha (not to mention Ben Grauer as The Narrator). Regisseur Dimitri Romanoff is Hilarion and stars like Ruth Ann Koesun populate the corps.

The dancers do well, given the obstacles, but because of its technical limitations this is not a good film to introduce general audiences to the ballet. It can be a treat for specialized audiences however.

**GISELLE.** 1956—Ulanova Version. See BOLSHOI BALLET. ?**

**GISELLE.** 98 min., 1964, b/w.**

*Rental $200 ($100 classroom) from Tricontinental.*

Alicia Alonso, Azari Plisetski, and the National Ballet of Cuba are featured in a full-length performance of the ballet.

GISELLE. 95 min., 1970, color. ?

*Information about availability from Dr. Klaus Hallig, International Trading Corporation, 919 Third Avenue, NYC 10022; (212) 838-2477.*

The American Ballet Theatre production featuring an outstanding cast: Erik Bruhn as Albrecht, Carla Fracci as Giselle, Toni Lander as Myrtha, and Bruce Marks as Hilarion, with Eleanor D'Antuono and Ted Kivitt dancing the *Peasant Pas de Deux*. There has been some rechoreographing for the film, and there are often maddening cuttings-away from the dancers, but the film still captures the story and the flavor reasonably well. Direction by Hugo Niebeling.

THE GOLDEN FLEECE. 25 min., color, silent. ?

*Rental probably from Bouchard, $30 or more.*

Hanya Holm as the element mercury in her work about alchemy, dominated by the theme and costumes of the surrealist painter Kurt Seligmann and the film approach of Thomas Bouchard. See Margaret Lloyd, *Borzoi Book of Modern Dance*, pp. 167-169. See also DREAM OF AN ALCHEMIST.

GRADUATION BALL. 27 min., 1949, b/w.*

*Rental $7.50 from Syracuse, $15 from Audio Brandon. Sale $175 from Audio Brandon.*

David Lichine's choreography is brightly rendered and acted by what then existed of De Basil's Original Ballet Russe. An intelligent and attractive film with excellent lighting. Featured dancers are Olga Morosova, Nina Stroganova, Vladimir Dokoudovsky, and Paul Grinwis.

THE GRAND CONCERT. 102 min., 1951, color.

*Rental $50 (higher for large audiences or where admission is charged) from Audio Brandon.*

Opera and ballet scenes with Galina Ulanova, Olga Lepeshinskaya, and others. Included are excerpts from *Swan Lake*, *Prince Igor*, and Lavrovsky's *Romeo and Juliet*.

GREAT BALLERINA. 6 min., 1950, b/w.

*Rental $5 from Illinois, $8.50 from Audio Brandon. Sale $40 from Dance Films, $85 from Macmillan.*

In an excerpt from the feature film RUSSIAN BALLERINA, Galina Ulanova performs most of the *Swan Lake* Act II adagio with Vladimir Preobrazhenski and the Bolshoi corps. The complete feature (not much of a film) is also available from Audio Brandon.

GREAT PERFORMANCE IN DANCE. 29 min., 1960, b/w.

*Rental $9.50 from Indiana, $11 from Association. Sale $125 from Indiana.*

A discussion with Walter Terry of performance styles and role interpretations. Brief clips include Anna Pavlova in the *Dying Swan* (with the wrong music superimposed), Irene and Vernon Castle, and Argentinita. Alexandra Danilova and Frederic Franklin then perform a duet from *Beau Danube* twice—once with the original Massine choreography, once with supposedly modernizing modifications by Walter Terry. Part of Martha Myers' "A Time to Dance" series.

HALPRIN.

A number of films by and about Ann Halprin, including a 1965 film of *Parades and Changes*, are available at rentals of around $35 from her Dancers' Workshop Company, 15 Ravine Way, Kentfield, CA 94904. See also PROCESSION.

HELEN TAMIRIS IN HER NEGRO SPIRITUALS. 16 min., 1959, b/w.*

*Rental $6.40 from Illinois, $7 from Penn State. Sale from Dance Films.*

Tamiris in her powerful modern dance solo classics: "Go Down Moses" (1932), "Swing Low, Sweet Chariot" (1929), "Git on Board, Lil' Chillun" (1932), "Crucifixion" (1930), and "Joshua Fit the Battle of Jericho" (1927). The first five minutes of the film are given over to an introduction by former *New York Times* dance critic, John Martin.

HISTORICAL FILMS. Box 46505, Hollywood, CA 90046; (213) 463-7111.

*Sells films from the historic (1894-1912) Library of Congress paper print collection for around $10 each.*

The motion picture quickly became a money-making enterprise after its invention late in the last century. The public was fascinated by the novelty and was eager to pump pennies and nickels into the peep-show machines that were used to display the early movies.

The makers and exhibitors of these films (among them, Thomas Edison himself) soon came to seek copyright protection for their profitable products and approached the logical agency—the Library of Congress. There was a problem, however. Early film stock was extremely unstable. One might obtain a print of the film for copyright purposes but find after a short time that the film had decomposed to dust while in a can perched on the shelf. Or the film might simply explode or burst into flame by spontaneous combustion, events even the most broadminded of librarians are likely to anticipate with a degree of distaste. The problem was essentially solved by requiring early filmmakers to make a "book" of any film they wanted to deposit for copyright. That is, the film would be copied, frame by frame, on long rolls of paper. This was the law between 1894 and 1912 and in that period great stocks of paper prints were placed at the Library of Congress.

As it happens, the great majority of these films soon ceased to exist in their original form. After they had had their public play they were generally allowed to decompose, burn, or explode, or were discarded before they could reach any of these states. But the paper prints are still there—some worn or frayed, but many still in fine shape. So, to reconstruct these early films which are now totally in public domain, all one has to do is re-photograph the paper prints, frame by frame, on modern film stock. The picture quality of the resulting film will not always be ideal, but the images will once again move as they did seventy years ago.

An extensive project to restore these old movies has been carried out and the resurrected clips and scraps contain many items of interest to dance people; early cameras seem to have been pointed at anything that moved which quite often included dancers. At least seventy-five of these early short movies were devoted to dance or dance-related subjects ranging from various forms of variety and vaudeville dancing (especially "skirt dancing") to ethnic and folk exhibitions (lots of cakewalking) to a trick film that may have included Isadora Duncan.

For samplings of some of these dance films, see EARLY DANCE FILMS and DANCE ON FILM: 1894-1912. A documentary film, THE FIRST FLICKERS (27 min., 1969, b/w) on the restoration of these historic films can be rented for $8.50 from Kent State or for $11 from Indiana. A comprehensive catalog of the entire paper print collection has been published: Kemp Niver's *Motion Pictures from the Library of Congress Paper Print Collection*. It sells for $35 from Historical Films and is available in many libraries.

## HOMMAGE A DEBUSSY. 65 min., 1962, b/w.

*Rental $20 from FACSEA.*
Marcel L'Herbier's interpretations with Ludmilla Tcherina and Serge Lifar.

## I AM A DANCER. 93 min., 1973, color. (Also available on 35mm, videocassette.)*

*Rental hundreds (probably thousands) of dollars from J. E. R. Pictures, 165 W. 46 Street, NYC 10036; (212) 247-4220.*
Four ballet segments featuring Rudolf Nureyev, interspersed with scenes of the dancer rehearsing, taking class, dressing, greeting his fans, reflecting on his life.

The segments include: 1) portions of Bournonville's *La Sylphide* (1836) in which a vacant and bewildered Nureyev is teamed with the soft and exquisite Carla Fracci; 2) a rehearsal with Deanne Bergsma of portions of Glen Tetley's tiresome *Field Figures* (to a Karlheinz Stockhausen score), with corrections by the choreographer; 3) a superb performance with Margot Fonteyn of the complete, or nearly complete, *Marguerite and Armand* choreographed for the pair in 1963 by Frederick Ashton (who comments briefly on the work); and 4) the *Sleeping Beauty Pas de Deux*, with a rather weak performance by Lynn Seymour, filmed on an empty stage.

The direction by Pierre Jourdan is generally adequate, though he has an almost charming penchant at times for naive gimmicks. Sections of *Marguerite and Armand* are seen mistily through a vaseline-ringed lens or rendered multiple by a kaleidoscopic device, *Field Figures* is cluttered with reaction shots, Nureyev's solo in *La Sylphide* is peppered with closeups of his fluttering legs.

## IMAGE, FLESH AND VOICE. 77 min., 1969, b/w.

*Rental $80 from FMC.*
A film by Ed Emshwiller described as "a non-story-telling feature film, a structural interplay of sound, image and sensual tensions." Features dancers Carolyn Carlson and Emery Hermans.

## IMMORTAL SWAN. 36 min., 1935, b/w.*

*Rental $30 from MOMA.*
After Anna Pavlova's death in 1931 her husband and manager, Victor Dandré, put together this compendium of films taken of her in various roles. The films, all from the 1920s, were originally shot silent and music was added under the direction of Aubrey Hitchins. Some home movie footage is also included.

The films were not always shot under good circumstances and they do not allow a full appreciation of the artist, but they do at least give us a glimpse of her theatricality and stage presence and of her rather brilliant technique. They also show her tastes in choreography and music and display some of her stage mannerisms, features sometimes criticized by her contemporaries.

Some of the original films were shot at 24 frames per second ("sound speed"), some at slower speeds closer to today's standard of "silent speed" (18 frames per second). In the listing of dance portions of the film below, projection speeds are suggested; in all cases the sound should be left *on*.

    1. *Chopiniana* (24 fps). Twelve women who had previously danced with Pavlova were assembled in the 1930s for the purposes of this film and open it by performing a limply romantic movement from her company's version of "Chopiniana" (choreography by Ivan Clustine).

    2. *Invitation to the Dance* (24 fps). Some waltzing by her company, then Pavlova's vivacious solo.

    3. *La Nuit* (24 fps). A solo of grief, choreography attributed to Nicholas Legat.

    4. *California Poppy* (24 fps). A rather improbable solo, choreographed by Pavlova.

    5. *Rondino* (24 fps). Various takes of this solo at various speeds, filmed outdoors.

    6. *Fairy Doll* (18 fps). Two impish solos; Pavlova plays the favorite doll of a toymaker.

    7. *Don Quixote* (18 fps). The full company in an adagio sequence from Act II. Pavlova is partnered by Pierre Vladimiroff.

    8. *Coquetteries de Columbine* (18 fps). A sparkling solo.

    9. *Danse Grecque* (18 fps). A draped, emotive, exotic solo reminiscent of Duncan or St. Denis.

    10. *Dragonfly* (24 fps). A famous solo choreographed by Pavlova.

For footage from Pavlova's version of *Dying Swan*, see BALLET FOR ALL—5. For further discussion, see *DM*, January 1976.

IMPULSES. 30 min., 1974, color.

*Rental $35, sale $400 from Impulses Foundation, 32 Jones Street, NYC 10014.*

Margaret Beals and Impulses Co. in performance. Investigates the art of improvisation.

IN A REHEARSAL ROOM. 11 min., 1975, color.*

*Rental $9 from Illinois. Rental $15, sale $250 from Otter Productions, 33 Riverside Drive, NYC 10023; (212) 580-9293.*

A lyrical, rhapsodic, romantic duet for Cynthia Gregory and Ivan Nagy, attractively filmed by David Hahn.

The dancers warm up in a sun-drenched ballet studio, casting shyly flirtatious glances at one other. Nagy touches Gregory on the shoulder, the music changes to Johann Pachelbel's beautiful "Canon in D," and the dancers launch into a duet—or a rehearsal of one—through which the flickering flirtation continues.

The dancing is everything one would expect from these two fine artists, and the choreography, by American Ballet Theatre's William Carter, is serviceable or better, depending on one's tolerance for the run-catch-clutch-and-swirl school of romantic duet-making.

For the most part filmmaker Hahn's camera stays fairly close in (but not usually close up) and is attentive to the lyrical flow of each dance phrase, although some are punctured with more cuts than seem entirely necessary. The photography is in a beautifully soft, slightly grainy color.

A book, also called *In a Rehearsal Room*, shows the making of the film. The photographs are by Susan Cook, the text by Robin Woodard. It is available from the publisher, Modernismo, 90 West Broadway, NYC 10007, or in bookstores for about $10. For more commentary on the film and for some of Cook's photographs, see *DM*, February 1976.

IN PRAISE OF FOLLY. 52 min., color.

*Rental $18.50 from Illinois. Rental $45, sale $525 from Audio Brandon.*

In this film we are asked to watch French choreographer Roland Petit as he muses about the follies of (other?) people and then presents brief ballets to illustrate them. The assorted "follies" are violence, publicity, machinery, power, and "count down," and there are two "escapes": love and drugs.

Based on a 1966 stage work, each tacky little ballet, long on sound and fury, desperately short on significance, is flashily photographed in beautiful color in studio settings incorporating the talents of various French sculptors and painters: Niki De Saint-Phalle, Martial Raysse, and Jean Tinguely. The film was written by Jean Cau. Petit directs and, in the least banal of the ballets, "Drugs," appears as a man trapped in the corner of an oppressively bare, white room.

Except for a few moments like this and for a brief glimpse of one of Tinguely's wonderful gigantic machines, the film would seem to have little value except as fuel for feminist groups. As in so much of Petit, there is a pronounced anti-feminist tone to this work. "Power," we are soberly told, "today is represented by women," and a picture is flashed of a female traffic cop. Then the "power" ballet shows us a group of men cavorting balletically with hideously bilious female-shaped balloons. To Chopin. That is about as witty as the film gets.

**INCENSE.** 5 min., 1953, color.**

*Rental $8, sale $80 from Rochester.*

Ruth St. Denis in her solo choreographed in 1906—sensuous, religious, and ecstatic, featuring the famous arm ripple. (An excerpt from RUTH ST. DENIS BY BARIBAULT.)

**INDEX.** 5 min., b/w.

*Rental $5, sale $50 from East End.*

A duet by Judith Dunn and Tony Holder is photographed in multiple exposure by Gene Friedman.

**INTRODUCTION TO DUNCAN DANCES.** 15 min., color.

*Rental $35, sale $235 from F. Randolph Associates, 1300 Arch Street, Philadelphia, PA 19107; (215) 567-0505.*

A recent filming of seven short Isadora Duncan choreographies badly danced (though the choreography is still legible) by Hortense Kooluris and a student group under the direction of Nadia Chilkovsky Nahumck.

Included are: 1) *Three Graces* (a trio to Schubert); 2) *Springtime* (choreography by Irma Duncan for children's group); 3) *Lullaby* (a lilting, cradling, naive but lovely, work to Schubert); 4) *Ecossaise* (a quintet to Schubert); 5) *Tanagra* (a rather dramatic trio to Corelli); 6) *Waltz Studies* (a goofy quintet to Strauss); and 7) *Scarf Dance* (rather coy, to Schubert).

**INVENTION IN DANCE.** 29 min., 1960, b/w.

*Rental $7.50 ($15 in East) from Utah, $7.70 from Iowa, $9.50 from Indiana, $11 from Association. Sale $125 from Indiana.*

A brief discussion with Alwin Nikolais about modern dance history including brief clips of Ruth St. Denis in *Radha* and of a pupil of Isadora Duncan. Nikolais demonstrates his approach to dance and discusses his interest in shapes, form, light, and sound.

Nikolais excerpts include *Noumenon* (three performers in all-encompassing sacks), *Web* (apparently an earlier version of *Tensile Involvement*, with big rubber bands), *Fixation* (a solo for Murray Louis), and *Discs* (a sextet in which each performer has a kind of garbage can lid on one foot). Please note that this film is in black and white and accordingly some of the Nikolais magic, which depends so much on color effects, is lost. Part of Martha Myers' "A Time to Dance" series.

**INVITATION TO THE DANCE.** 93 min., 1956, color.

*Rental $100 from Films Inc.*

Gene Kelly and his choreography are featured in this all-dance, MGM feature. Also seen: Igor Youskevitch, Claire Sombert, Tamara Toumanova, and Diana Adams. The three ballets are "Circus," "Ring Around the Rosy," and "Sinbad the Sailor."

**J MARKS.** A series of films.

*Rental $12.50 to $30 from Audio Brandon.*

Films featuring the San Francisco Contemporary Dancers Company. Includes FIRE SERMON, CEREMONY OF INNOCENCE, LANDSCAPE OF THE BODY, NIGHT IS A SORCERESS, DESIRE, ORACLE OF THE BRANCH, A SEASON IN HELL, KAMA SUTRAS.

**JOHN CRANKO.** 7 min., 1970, color.

*Rental free from Modern Talking Picture Service.*

A documentary, in English, on the late choreographer and director of the Stuttgart Ballet. Includes interview material and practice sessions with Marcia Haydée and Richard Cragun.

**JUNCTION.** 12 min., 1965, color.**

*Rental $14 from Rochester. Rental $20, sale $250 from Rudy Burckhardt, 50 W. 29 Street, NYC 10001.*

A splendid film of a brilliant 1961 work by Paul Taylor contrasting quick-paced "scribbling" movements with tranquil processionals.

In a chipper and informative essay he contributed to Selma Jeanne Cohen's valuable book, *The Modern Dance: Seven Statements of Belief*, Taylor discusses the dance style he used in *Junction*, relating it to action painting: "dance scribbling," he calls it. "The idea is to see action rather than shape or line. It works best for fast movement. . .If [the dancers] are doing it right, the viewer says: 'This is something! But what is it?'"

There are really two central movement themes or motifs in *Junction*: The severely agitated "scribbling" style (seen most typically with the dancers bent over at the waist, their arms flailing behind them) and a very serene processional pacing. Both are introduced in the opening solo for Taylor: he walks calmly toward the audience, bursts suddenly into a flurry of movement as the music begins, and then, just as abruptly, resumes his stolid pacing.

It is the contrast between these two kinds of movement and the brusque transitions from one extreme movement state to the other ("tranquillity" and "turmoil" Taylor calls them in an early program note) that seem to have inspired the work's title. There is also a more literal suggestion of a junction when various dancer parades are arranged on near collision course as they intersect down stage diagonals.

For music Taylor uses movements from Johann Sebastian Bach's first and fourth suites for unaccompanied cello. None of the movements chosen is slow. One is a rather quiet, even lyrical, minuet to which Taylor sets a brief lilting duet and an exquisite procession in which the men gently trade off a burden (Carolyn Adams, sitting upright) among them. The rest of the music ranges from the active to the frantic (though Bach probably never thought of it as scribbling). Taylor is very aware of the music, but he deals with it freely, occasionally letting the choreography mirror the music quite closely, but mostly striving for contrast and visual counterpoint—some of the calmest dancing is counterposed with some of the most agitated music.

For all its energetic scribbling, *Junction* is tightly structured. Not only is the turmoil-tranquillity theme carefully thought through, but there are neatly crafted transitions between sections of the work and the finale, a beautiful shifting processional cluster, evolves at the end to an image seen in the opening movement of the work: a man huddled on the floor with a woman standing on his back.

In its earliest performances, *Junction* included some Dadaesque use of props—a bedsheet was brought on stage and meticulously folded, for example. By the time the film was made, four years after the premiere, these portions of the dance had apparently been eliminated; at any rate they don't appear on the film. Nor is there an onstage cellist as in some performances.

Filmmaker Rudy Burckhardt has done an excellent job in capturing this fine dance work. The lighting and exposure speed are such that the fastest dartings and squigglings and flailings of Taylor's dancers become something of a blur on the film, an effect which actually serves to heighten the kinetic point Taylor is exploring in much of the choreography. There are a few places where the dancers get out of the frame, and the camera might have been placed higher in the second movement the better to show the diagonal processions, but such defects are quite minor.

The film was shot silent with the music from the Taylor company's tape added later, so there may be places where the dancing and music get out of sync a bit, particularly toward the ends of movements. But Taylor's choreography in this work rarely seems to require precise synchronization and, if there is a problem with sync, it doesn't seem to harm the impact of the work.

The beautiful costumes for *Junction*, with broad patches of bright color, are by Alex Katz. The dancers on the film, all in fine form, are Bettie de Jong, Carolyn Adams, Dan Wagoner, Elizabeth Walton, Jane Kosminsky, Molly Moore, Daniel Williams, and Taylor.

LAMENT. 18 min., 1951, b/w.

*Rental $4.70 from Northern Illinois, $5.70 from Southern Illinois, $7 from Penn State, $10 from Syracuse.*

Doris Humphrey's tribute to a dying bullfighter, based on a poem by Federico Garcia Lorca, is rather clumsily photographed by Walter Strate with the original cast: José Limón as the Bullfighter, Letitia Ide as the Figure of Destiny, Ellen Love as the Figure of a Woman. For a helpful discussion of this work, see Margaret Lloyd, *Borzoi Book of Modern Dance*, pp. 123-125. Humphrey's scenario is printed in Selma Jeanne Cohen, *Doris Humphrey*, pp. 242-247.

LAMENTATION. 10 min., 1943, color.*

*Rental $5 from Illinois, $9 from Penn State, $10 (members only) from Dance Films. Sale $69.10 from Audiovisual Archives, National Archives and Records Service, Washington, D.C. 20408.*

A film interpretation, by Mr. and Mrs. Simon Moselsio, of Martha Graham in her 1930 solo of mourning.

As Leroy Leatherman puts it (*Martha Graham*, p. 119), the film is "a pastiche of poses she did for a sculptor, not the dance at all." But it remains the only available film showing Graham at that stage in her career. John Martin also appears on the film discussing modern dance, as does Louis Horst, providing the piano accompaniment. For a complete performance of the solo by Peggy Lyman, see MARTHA GRAHAM DANCE COMPANY.

THE LANGUAGE OF DANCE. 29 min., 1960, b/w.

*Rental $7.50 ($15 in East) from Utah, $9.50 from Indiana, $11 from Association. Sale $125 from Indiana.*

A discussion with José Limón about the language of movement. Limón and his company then perform extensive excerpts from his *There Is a Time* (1958).

The dancers include Pauline Koner, Lucas Hoving, Betty Jones, Lucy Venable, Lola Huth, Harlan McCallum, Chester Wolenski, and Robert Powell. Part of Martha Myers' "A Time to Dance" series.

LIFE STAR. 20 min., 1965, b/w.

*Rental $6 ($12 in the East) from Utah.*

Master's thesis film by Shirley White Nelson.

LIGHT, PART 5.  20 min., 1976, color.**

*Rental $16, sale $260 from Rochester. Also available from Illinois.*

An extraordinary trio from 1971 by avant-garde choreographer Kei Takei. Takei's works are mostly unspecific rituals that can be delicate or violent, high-spirited or doom-laden. Her major work is called *Light*. It consists, so far, of thirteen varied parts which, on those occasions when they are performed in sequence, last many hours.

The film shows *Light, Part 5*, a slow, liquid trio that takes place in an isolated pool of light. The work is carefully structured. The two men (Maldwyn Pate and John de Marco) evolve into sixteen different poses. In each of these one of the men is limp while the other supports him. At the end of each pose, the supporting man slowly weakens (starting with the face) until the two collapse to the floor. Then they slowly move into the next pose with the opposite man taking the supporting role. Meanwhile, the woman (Takei) has her own correlated ritual consisting of three elements: leaning far back facing upward, adhering to the sculpted poses of the men, and collapsing to the ground.

Images projected by the trio are left up to the viewer and the descriptive words applied by observers have varied widely. Directed by Neelon Crawford

LIGHT, PART 5

and John Mueller. For commentary on Takei's work, see *Dance Scope*, Spring 1975.

LILEYA.  88 min., 1960, color.

*Rental $50 (higher for large audiences or where admission is charged) from Audio Brandon.*

A Ukrainian ballet about young love in eighteenth-century Russia. Features Yevgenia Yershova. Narrated in English.

LIMBO.  Color.*

*Information from Ed Emshwiller, 43 Red Maple Drive North, Wantagh, NY 11793; (516) 735-6688.*

A film by Ed Emshwiller featuring the Alwin Nikolais Company.

THE LITTLE HUMPBACKED HORSE.  85 min., 1961, color.*

*Rental $55 from Audio Brandon.*

Maya Plisetskaya, Vladimir Vasiliev, Alexander Radunsky, Anya Scherbinina, and the Bolshoi Ballet corps and orchestra are featured in this fairytale ballet to music of Rodion Shchedrin with choreography by Radunsky.

Maya Plisetskaya and corps in THE LITTLE HUMPBACKED HORSE

MAGIC FIDDLE.  16 min., 1956, color.

*Rental $7 from USC.*

A pleasant folk-tale ballet danced by members of the Norwegian Ballet. Choreography by Gerd Kjolass.

MAKING OF A BALLET:  RUDI VAN DANTZIG— A CHOREOGRAPHER AND HIS WORLD.  60 min., early 1970s, color.?*

*Rental free probably from Films of the Nations, 7820 20th Avenue, Brooklyn, NY 11214.*

A reasonably diverting documentary on van Dantzig and the Netherlands National Ballet showing rehearsals and bits from a staged performance of van Dantzig's *Painted Birds*, a highly theatrical, neo-Béjart ballet featuring masks, massed bodies, grotesque costumes, and a heavy message about the "fallibility of human relationships." At the end of the ballet, the dancers are required to sing a Bach chorus and do so, very well.

Backstage jumpiness is depicted and there is a somewhat pompous narration that reviews van Dantzig's choreographic output and point of view.

## MAN WHO DANCES: EDWARD VILLELLA. 54 min., color. X

This documentary stresses the pain and exhaustion that are so much a part of the professional ballet dancer's life. It has been withdrawn, although a copy does lurk in the New York State Library in Albany (usable only in New York State, but not by educational institutions—see p. 4) and perhaps elsewhere. For a partial substitute, see BALLET WITH EDWARD VILLELLA.

## MARGOT FONTEYN. 54 min., 1970, color.**

*Rental $22 from Illinois. Rental $60, sale $675 from Audley Square, P.O. Box 134, Old Greenwich, CT 06870.*

An attractive documentary on the great ballerina, written and directed by Keith Money.

About two-thirds of the film is given over to a well-paced biographical sketch. Fonteyn is seen rehearsing, taking class, buying clothes, rushing through airports, greeting prospective donors to the Royal Academy of Dance, giving a backstage tour to Princess Margaret, working out in an empty studio, looking at funny photographs in her dressing room. There are also extensive scenes showing her relaxing in Panama with her invalid husband. She is seen swimming, boating, watching parades, greeting the neighbors.

Through these scenes an engagingly conversational narration is supplied, principally by Fonteyn and by her mother, discussing the dancer's childhood, training, and career, and her approach to life and to the dance art. Her extraordinary dancing partnership with Rudolf Nureyev is assessed frankly. The commentary seems candid and intelligent; a picture emerges of a dedicated, poised, hard-working professional, not easily ruffled, with an unmuddled understanding of her place in the dance world and a certain sense of humor about it.

Interpolated into this documentary material are several dance excerpts, the most important of which is a complete performance of the eight-minute "Rose Adagio" from Petipa's *Sleeping Beauty*. Fonteyn's

Princess Aurora is, of course, legendary and the secure, radiant, theater-filling performance she gives on this film shows why. The ballet excerpt was filmed on stage with a full cast at the Pavilion Theatre in England.

Also of great interest is footage from a rehearsal of the exquisite pas de deux from Frederick Ashton's *Birthday Offering*, partnered by Nureyev. As David Vaughan points out in his book, *Frederick Ashton and His Ballets*, the duet is something of a tour de force, relying almost not at all on lifts. The dancers run through the duet on a bare stage to piano music, but in full costume. There is a missed connection at the final pose and Fonteyn, unsupported, crumples to the floor in a very poised and very pretty heap. The choreographer makes some corrections and clarifications and the dancers repeat the ending—correctly this time. Another, briefer, rehearsal excerpt shows Fonteyn and David Wall in portions of the adagio and conclusion of *Swan Lake*, Act II.

The other major dance excerpt on the film is the adagio, female variation, and coda from the romantic and rather frolicsome *Gayaneh Pas de Deux* (choreography uncredited) in which Fonteyn is partnered by Viktor Rona of the Hungarian State Opera. The duet was filmed in a studio with a heavy and rather pointless use of double exposures and lingering dissolves.

## MARGOT FONTEYN IN LES SYLPHIDES. 8 min., 1947, b/w.

*Rental $5 from Em Gee, $8 from Rochester. Sale $31 from Thunderbird.*

An excerpt from the British feature, *Little Ballerina*. The light and lyrical Fonteyn with Michael Somes and corps is seen on stage dancing the first movement of *Les Sylphides*. The dancing scenes are intercut with dialogue scenes from backstage.

Most useful in connection with a showing of EVENING WITH THE ROYAL BALLET, the 1963 feature that includes a complete performance of the ballet with Fonteyn and Rudolf Nureyev.

## MARTHA GRAHAM DANCE COMPANY. 89 min., 1976, color.**

*Rental $27, sale $665 from Indiana.*

This generally excellent program from the "Dance in America" series features five complete Graham works plus an excerpt from a sixth, each introduced briefly and interestingly by Graham: 1) The ebullient *Diversion of Angels* (1948) danced by a cast led by Peggy Lyman and Peter Sparling (white couple), Takako Asakawa and David Hatch Walker (red couple), and Elisa Monte and Tim Wengerd (yellow couple); 2) *Lamentation* (1930), a solo of mourning, danced by Lyman; 3) the exuberant solo *Frontier*

(1935), danced by Janet Eilber; 4) *Adorations* (1975), a rather bland work for the company demonstrating the state of Graham technique in the 1970s; 5) Medea's dance of vengeance from *Cave of the Heart* (1946), performed by Asakawa; and 6) *Appalachian Spring* (1944) danced by Yuriko Kimura as the bride with Wengerd as the husbandman, Hatch Walker as the preacher, Eilber as the pioneer woman, and Jessica Chao, Bonnie Oda Homsey, Lucinda Mitchell, and Elisa Monte as the worshippers. The program is introduced by celebrity Gregory Peck who renders some overblown prose written by Nancy Hamilton.

Takako Asakawa and David Hatch Walker in *Adorations* from MARTHA GRAHAM DANCE COMPANY

The direction by Merrill Brockway is mostly thoughtful, intelligent, and sensitive, although *Lamentation* and the *Cave of the Heart* excerpt are hampered by some unnecessary closeups, and *Diversion of Angels* is troubled by some disorienting cuts to side cameras, by a tendency to telegraph or obscure entrances, and by too much reliance on the distance-exaggerating wide-angle lens. The transfer from videotape to film is rather good, though some scenes seem a little dark.

There are some excellent performances on the film, particularly in *Diversion of Angels* and *Adorations*. The performance of *Frontier* seems to reflect Graham's mid-1970s perspective on some of her early dances: the solo is speeded up (a 1964 record film shows a performance nearly fourteen percent slower) and the simple elemental point of the work, the

soloist's exhilaration at the challenge of space, seems cloaked almost embarrassedly in a veneer of decorative frolic.

A comparison of this filmed version of *Appalachian Spring* with the 1958 film APPALACHIAN SPRING is a fascinating exercise. (For some suggestions about simultaneous projection, see p. 15.) The 1976 version shows relatively few changes in choreography, but rather remarkable differences in characterization. In general the 1976 version is more athletically flamboyant, more decorative, more effusively and ingratiatingly theatrical. What gets lost is some of the directness, simplicity, and careful, unhurried articulation that can make this dance masterpiece so deeply moving.

The central role, of course, is that of the bride. As Graham notes in her introduction to the work in the "Dance in America" program, the dance is primarily joyous "but there are moments of darkness too." It is the bride who expresses this duality best. At times she fairly bubbles over with a dizzy, giddy joyousness as she skitters in happy anticipation of her life on the frontier—marriage, creating a home, children to come. At the same time there is fear; the sheer vastness of the space is an awesome, even terrifying, challenge. And she may be concerned that the children she yearns for can only come through the painful and dangerous process of childbirth.

This contrast is expressed principally in two passages for the bride. One is an extraordinary solo in the last half of the work in which playful, carefree steps are alternated with passages suggesting fear and prayerful foreboding. The other is at the very end as the bride gazes out uncertainly at the surrounding space and then backs away from it, seeking bounded refuge in the warmth and safety of her new home.

Yuriko Kimura in the 1976 film expresses the giddy side of the bride better than Graham, then sixty-four years old, was able to in the 1958 film. But what is largely missing in Kimura's bride is the darker aspect of the character and, accordingly, a major point of the dance work is missing. It is clear from a direct comparison of the films that the steps are essentially unaltered. But where Graham clearly, if subtly, articulated the two sides of the bride, Kimura tends to blur the differences and is unable to project the darker side distinctly.

There are also important differences in the relationship between the bride and her husband. In both cases there is love and mutual respect, but the Graham/Hodes relationship in the 1958 film is more stolid and archetypal, the Kimura/Wengerd relationship more fawning and cuddly. Part of this can be seen in the bride's solos when the other characters freeze in poses around the stage as she dances around and up to them. In the 1976 version, Graham has

Wengerd break out of his frozen position to smile at and to gesture lovingly toward his bride as she cavorts near him. It's an odd change; why does he physically break into her thoughts this way while the others do not?

Bertram Ross' preacher in the 1958 version is brilliantly characterized, a carefully articulated blend of pompous self-righteousness and systematic humbug. Every pose, every inclination of the head, every gesture seems to have been fully thought through. David Hatch Walker is one of the finest of Graham dancers (as are Kimura and Wengerd), but he does not give the role the happy inflections characteristic of Ross' performance. For example, there is a wonderful passage where the preacher, having struck a stern pose, is reluctantly but uncontrollably urged into a frolicsome little dance by a bubbling melody in the score: first his shoulders catch the rhythm, then his head, and soon his whole body. Ross does this clearly and cleanly; Walker blurs it.

A couple of choreographic differences are worth specific mention. Freudian symbolism apparently lost some of its hold on Graham's theatrical sense between 1958 and 1976. In the earlier version, there is a sequence where the bride, envisioning marriage, strokes the phallic back of the chair and then leans back dreamily on the floor. The gesture is missing in the later film.

Another change occurs at the ending. In both cases the bride, retreating into the house, seats herself on the chair; her husband places his hand on her shoulder and she places her hand on his. In the 1958 version, she then slowly raises her free arm, gesturing toward the vast space outside. Although the 1976 version is less "dark" in general than the 1958 version, in this case the reverse is true: instead of gesturing toward the space, Graham has the bride in the later version simply turn her head slowly to gaze out at it. It is quite an unsettling image, even a rather scary one. Regrettably, Brockway somewhat muddies the effect by choosing to dissolve to a double image at that point—an unfortunate flaw in an otherwise quite excellent photographic presentation.

MARY WIGMAN: FOUR SOLOS. 10 min., 1929, b/w.*

*Rental $13 from Rochester, $15 from MOMA. Sale $150 from MOMA.*

An early sound film showing Wigman performing three solos from the *Shifting Landscape* cycle, choreographed in 1929: the ecstatic *Seraphic Song*, the languorous *Pastoral*, and the joyous *Dance of Summer*. The film concludes with Wigman in portions of the famous *Witch Dance* of 1926.

The first three solos emphasize Wigman's lyrical, joyous side while the *Witch Dance* shows the better known side, the dances that were "an ecstasy of gloom, stressing the demonic and macabre, as if to exorcise through movement the secret evils in man's nature," as Margaret Lloyd put it in a brilliant essay in her *Borzoi Book of Modern Dance* thirty years ago. The *Witch Dance* shows the dancer in a stark, gaunt mask, sheathed in a brocade wrap. The dance, as seen on film, is done in a sitting position on the floor, the hands and arms clawing the air, the body dragged on its haunches menacingly toward the camera.

The film does not show the complete *Witch Dance*. Descriptions and photographs show sections with the dancer at full height, glowering at the audience, her arms stretched overhead. The dance is rather fully described in words with pictures, floor patterns, and a sketch of the music in Rudolf Bach's 1933 book, *Das Mary Wigman Werk*. For a free copy of an English translation of the description, send a stamped, self-addressed envelope to Wigman Dance, Dance Film Archive, University of Rochester, Rochester, NY 14627.

For a further discussion of the solos, see Wigman's *The Language of Dance*. For a discussion of the film, see *DM*, March 1976.

The *Witch Dance* from MARY WIGMAN: FOUR SOLOS

MENSCH UND KUNSTFIGUR (MAN AND MASK: OSKAR SCHLEMMER AND THE "BAUHAUS" STAGE). 28 min., 1968, color.*

*Rental free from German Consulate General, 460 Park Avenue, NYC 10022; (212) 688-3523. Also from Modern Talking Picture Service.*

An intelligent documentary on Schlemmer's work and philosophy. Includes extensive demonstrations of Schlemmer's patterned dances using poles, lighted circles, cubes, masks, panels.

The dances, mostly from the 1926 work, *Dances for the Experimental Stage*, include *Metal Dance*, *Space Dance*, *Form Dance*, *Gesture Dance*, *Pole Dance*, *Hoop Dance*, *Flats Dance*, *Game of Bricks*, and *Chorus of Masks*. See *Dance Perspectives* No. 41 and Walter Gropius (ed.), *The Theater of the Bauhaus*. Ballet master: Hannes Winkler; music: Erick Ferstl. See also TRIADISCHE BALLETT.

MERCE CUNNINGHAM. 13 min., 1964, b/w.

*Rental $6.40 from Illinois, $8.50 from Penn State, $12.50 from Audio Brandon. Sale $140 from Audio Brandon.*

Less than adequate, this film fragmentarily documents the Merce Cunningham Dance Company in rehearsal and performance in France during their 1964 world tour.

MERCE CUNNINGHAM. 29 min., half-inch videotape. ?

*Rental $25, purchase on request probably from Campus Film Distributors Corp., 20 E. 46 Street, NYC 10017.*

The choreographer demonstrates his theories in an interview.

MIDSUMMER NIGHT'S DREAM. 93 min., 1967, color, Panavision.**

*Rental information from Harry K. McWilliams, 151 Lafayette Street, NYC 10013; (212) 925-5013. May also be available from Opera Presentations, 75 Maiden Lane, NYC 10038; (212) 269-3430.*

A superb film (but read on) of George Balanchine's magical two-act 1962 ballet based on Shakespeare's play using music by Felix Mendelssohn.

Filmed in June 1966 featuring New York City Ballet dancers Suzanne Farrell as Titania, Edward Villella as Oberon, Arthur Mitchell as Puck, Allegra Kent and Jacques d'Amboise as the Court Dancers, and Patricia McBride, Nicholas Magallanes, Mimi Paul, and Roland Vazquez as the mortal lovers. Direction and screen adaptation by Balanchine and Dan Eriksen.

The film is available, expensively, on 35mm in its intended wide-screen Panavision version and it looks glorious that way. The 16mm prints (also expensive), however, are scanned—that is, the sides of the picture are lopped off to reduce it to the usual size. In the process, of course, much of the choreography is lost, particularly where full chorus is used. In some scenes, dancers bound right out of the frame. So, while the film is highly recommended in its 35mm version, the same cannot be said for the 16mm version until wide-screen prints are available in that format.

Other dancers featured are Gloria Govrin as Hippolyta, Francisco Moncion as Theseus, Conrad Ludlow as Titania's cavalier, Richard Rapp as Bottom, and Suki Shorer as First Butterfly. Karinska's stage costumes are used, but the sets have been rede-signed by Howard Bay and are a considerable improvement over the David Hays sets used in the stage version. An article on the making of the film appears in *DM*, August 1966.

MISS JULIE. 37 min., 1964, b/w. See SWEDEN: FIRE AND ICE.**

MODERN BALLET. 29 min., 1960, b/w.*

*Rental $7 from UCLA, $9.50 from Indiana, $11 from Association. Sale $125 from Indiana.*

A discussion with Antony Tudor about psychological insights in dance and about changes in ballet suggested by his work and by that of Fokine.

Hugh Laing and Nora Kaye demonstrate with moments from Tudor's *Lilac Garden, Gala Performance, Pillar of Fire, Romeo and Juliet, Dim Lustre*, and *Undertow*. They also perform longer duets from *Pillar of Fire* (the seduction of Hagar) and *Romeo and Juliet* (Romeo's departure into exile), and Tudor dances a brief duet with Kaye from *Pillar of Fire*. Also shown in passing is a 1913 clip of the famous Moscow ballerina Yekaterina Geltzer (1876-1962) frolicking about with the mustachioed Vasily Tichomiroff. Part of Martha Myers' "A Time to Dance" series.

A complete performance of *Pillar of Fire* (with Sallie Wilson) appears on AMERICAN BALLET THEATRE: A CLOSE-UP IN TIME, and makes an interesting comparison (see p. 21).

THE MOISEYEV DANCERS IN "THE STROLLERS." 6 min., 1952, color.

*Rental $4 from USC, $8.50 from Audio Brandon. Sale $110 from Audio Brandon.*

Also available on CONCERT OF STARS.

MOON DANCES (Eleanor King). See SHE AND MOON DANCES.

MOOR'S PAVANE. 16 min., 1950, color.

*Rental $6 from South Florida, $7.50 ($15 in East) from Utah, $8.50 from Boston, $11 from Penn State, $11 from Syracuse, $15 from Audio Brandon. Sale $195 from Audio Brandon.*

José Limón's great work, which filters the story of Othello through a series of stylized court dances, in a film version by Walter Strate. Limón dances the role of Othello, Lucas Hoving is Iago, Betty Jones is Desdemona, and Ruth Currier is Emilia.

The work is not presented complete on the film. Emilia's part is substantially reduced and all the material after Desdemona's death (Emilia's revelation to the Moor of Iago's deception, Othello's collapse on his wife's corpse) is deleted. Also, some ponderously enunciated lines from Shakespeare are needlessly superimposed, mostly at the beginning and, destructively, the end. There are also some filmic repetitions of movement that are not in musical sync.

MORNING STAR (CHOLPON). 75 min., 1961, color.

*Rental $60 from Audio Brandon.*
A ballet legend from Central Asia danced by the Kirghizan State Opera Ballet.

MOSCOW BALLET SCHOOL. 19 min., 1973, color.

*Rental $18, sale $140 from Audio Brandon.*
Documentary on the Moscow Academic School of Choreography.

MOTION (Murray Louis). See DANCE AS AN ART FORM.

MOVE! 29 min., 1974, color.

*Rental $50, sale $215 from Steeg.*
Sue Cambigue and Bella Lewitsky in a Reno elementary school as part of the Artists in Schools program.

MOVE IT! 19 min., color.

*Rental, sale probably from Radim.*
Zany film featuring the Ririe-Woodbury Dance Company.

NAGRIN. 10 min., 1967, color.

*Rental $10, sale $120 from Idyllwild School of Music and the Arts, University of Southern California, Idyllwild, CA 92349.*
Daniel Nagrin dances two solos in the mountains of California: *The Path* and *A Gratitude*.

NAGRIN.

*A number of film and videotape programs by Daniel Nagrin are available for rental and sale from Nagrin Dance Foundation, 550 Broadway, NYC 10012; (212) 677-9188.*

NANA and THE EXERCISES WHICH MADE A WORLD FAMOUS BALLERINA OF NANA GOLLNER. ?

*Probably available from Erik Cooper, 1355 North Gardner, No. 101, West Hollywood, CA 90046.*
Two films on Nana Gollner. See also *DM*, October 1973, p. 6.

NEW DANCE—RECORD FILM. 30 min., 1978, color.*

*Rental $22, sale $360 from Rochester.*
Doris Humphrey's extraordinary modern dance classic of affirmation, choreographed in 1935. This is a *record film* (single, fixed camera) of the 1972 reconstruction as performed by the professional Repertory Company at the American Dance Festival at Connecticut College.

The popular last section of the work, VARIATIONS AND CONCLUSION (also available as a separate film), was reconstructed from Labanotation. The rest came from the memories of Charles Weidman, Edith Orcutt, and Beatrice Seckler. Weidman is responsible for the "Third Theme" for the men's group which he had choreographed in the original version and for the "Prelude," a duet originally for himself and Humphrey which no one could remember at all. Linda Tarnay dances Humphrey's role, Peter Woodin, Weidman's. Music by Wallingford Riegger. For Humphrey's commentary on *New Dance*, see Selma Jeanne Cohen's *Doris Humphrey: An Artist First* or her *Dance as a Theatre Art*. For suggestions about showing this film, see p. 9.

NIGHT JOURNEY. 29 min., 1961, b/w.**

*Rental $7.50 from South Florida, $7.50 ($15 in East) from Utah, $8.90 from Illinois, $9.40 from Michigan, $9.45 from Iowa, $10 from Kent State, $11 from Penn State, $13 from Syracuse, $15 from Audio Brandon, $18 from California, $25 from Phoenix. Sale $250 from Phoenix.*
Martha Graham's brilliant and powerful retelling of the Oedipus legend, expertly filmed. Music by William Schuman, sets by Isamu Noguchi. Graham is Jocasta, Bertram Ross is Oedipus, Paul Taylor is Tiresias, and Helen McGehee the leader of the chorus which consists of Ethel Winter, Mary Hinkson, Linda Hodes, Akiko Kanda, Carol Payne, and Bette Shaler. Directed by Alexander Hammid.

Extended analytic notes by John Mueller for this film are available from American Dance Guild, 152 W. 42 Street, NYC 10036. A film of Sophocles' play OEDIPUS REX featuring Christopher Plummer can be rented for $100 from Swank or from Universal/16.

NINE VARIATIONS ON A DANCE THEME. 13 min., 1967, b/w.*

*Rental $5.50 from Kent State, $6.10 from Michigan, $6.90 from Illinois, $10 from UCLA, $10 from USC, $14 from California, $15 from FMC. Sale from Radim.*
In this highly imaginative film a dancer (Bettie de Jong of the Paul Taylor Company) repeats a single pattern: she rises from the floor to full height and

then spirals back down to lie on the floor once again. The variations are for the camera and each one captures the movement in a different way: circling the dancer, gyrating, concentrating on a single body part, cutting backward and forward in time, etc.

The filmmaker, Hilary Harris, discusses the film in *Dance Perspectives* No. 30, pp. 44-47. For other films by Mr. Harris, see the Radim and FMC catalogs.

## THE NUTCRACKER. 60 min., 1967, color.

*Rental $40 from Audio Brandon, $40 from Association, $75 from Swank, $75 from Warner Bros. Film Gallery, 4000 Warner Boulevard, Burbank, CA 91522, (212) 841-1500.*

A rather gaudy German production. Kurt Jacob provides choreography to supplement Lev Ivanov's original, and in the middle Petipa's *Bluebird Pas de Deux* (from the *Sleeping Beauty*) is inserted.

The final pas de deux between, in this version, the Nutcracker (Edward Villella) and the Sugar Plum Fairy (Melissa Hayden—the Nutcracker's mother, says the narrator) can be compared to George Balanchine's version from the 1950s recorded by Hayden and Jacques d'Amboise in the film, A TIME TO DANCE. Niels Kehlet and Helga Heinrich dance the Bluebird duet. At least on some prints, there are problems with the sound synchronization, particularly on the variations and coda of the Sugar Plum Fairy duet. Harald Kreutzberg appears as "Dr. Hoffmann" (a.k.a. Herr Drosselmeyer).

## THE OFFICIAL DOCTRINE. 3 min., 1967, b/w.

*Rental $5, sale $50 from East End.*
A solo by Judith Dunn in photography by Gene Friedman.

## OLGA. 48 min., 1973, color.*

*Rental $21 from Illinois, $22.30 from Michigan.*
Documentary on Soviet Olympic gymnast, Olga Korbut.

## OLYMPIA DIVING SEQUENCE. 4 min., 1937, b/w.**

*Rental $5 from South Florida, $7.50 from Kit Parker, $7.50 from Budget, $10 from California, $10 from Audio Brandon, $10 from Syracuse, $15 from Viewfinders. Rental $15, sale $70 from Phoenix.*
Famous sequence from Leni Riefenstahl's classic "Olympia."

## ON EDGE. ?

*A rather poor color film of a rooftop piece by Elizabeth Keen may possibly be obtained from Teletactics, Inc., 9 E. 19 Street, NYC 10003.*

## ON WINGS OF SONG. 15 min., 1955, b/w.

*Rental $5 from Syracuse, $10 from Audio Brandon. Sale $110 from Audio Brandon.*
Vienna Boys Choir sings Schubert, Brahms, Herbeck, and Mozart, some of which accompanies a ballet choreographed by Toni Birkmeyer.

## OPUS. 29 min., 1967, color.*

*Rental $12 from Illinois, $30 from Pyramid. Sale $375 from Pyramid.*
An impressionistic survey of the contemporary arts in Britain. The film includes a performance by Anthony Dowell, Vyvyan Lorrayne, and Robert Mead of one movement from Ashton's *Monotones II*, set to one of Satie's *Gymnopédies*. Ashton is seen rehearsing the dancers in this same piece in the film, BEHIND THE SCENES WITH THE ROYAL BALLET.

On the rest of the film are glimpses of paintings by Francis Bacon and Alan Davie, jewelry by Gerda Flockinger, sculpture by Henry Moore and Eduardo Paolozzi, fashions by Mary Quant, architecture by Colin St. John Wilson, *Marat/Sade* by Peter Brook, *Hamlet* by David Warner, *The Homecoming* by Harold Pinter, music by Benjamin Britten.

## OPUS OP. 20 min., 1967, color.

*Rental $13.50 from Syracuse. Rental $25, sale $240 probably from BFA.*
A documentary on a performance of Anna Sokolow's *Opus 65* by the City Center Joffrey Ballet and the Crome Syrcus (plus a light show) at a tiny-stage theater in Seattle. Comments and reactions by the audience are included.

## ORFEUS AND JULIE. 6 min., 1970, color.

*Rental free from Danish Information Office, 280 Park Avenue, NYC 10017 and from Royal Danish Consulate General in Los Angeles or Chicago.*
Two dancers and multiple images. Routine, if colorful.

ORION DANCE FILMS, 614 Davis Street, Evanston, IL 60201, is distributing ten films which feature the Gus Giordano Dance Company or the Illinois Ballet Company (doing *Coppélia* Act II and Anton Dolin's *Pas de Quatre* among other things). Each film is about 28 min. long.  Two are in color and rent for $35, sell for $350; the others rent for $25, sell for $250.

## OUT OF CHAOS: JEAN ERDMAN. 13 min., 1967, b/w.

*Rental $6.10 from Illinois.*
A subjective documentary of the dancer, choreographer, and playwright, made while she was visiting artist-in-residence at UCLA.  Erdman performs excerpts from dances spanning her career.  Conversations, class sessions shown.

## PAKHITA (PAQUITA).  23 min., 1940s, b/w.*

*Rental $13, sale $140 from Audio Brandon.*
Excerpts from the sparkling Petipa ballet brightly danced by soloists of the Maly Ballet of Leningrad.

## PARACELSUS. 102 min., 1943, b/w.

*Rental $35, lease $600, from Trans-World Films, 332 South Michigan Avenue, Chicago, IL 60604; (312) 992-1530.*
A rather leaden medieval drama made in Germany during World War II.  It incorporates, however, the theatrical talents of German dance-mime, Harald Kreutzberg.

His role is a fairly small one but accounts for by far the best scene in the film.  He plays a mischievous, mute, disease-bearing jester or juggler who has accidentally been smuggled into a town barricaded against outsiders because of the plague. He comes to a noisy, crowded beer-hall and leads the mob in a compulsive dance of death—a horrible, convulsive, hypnotic ritual—until he collapses senseless.  Thus the scene begins on a raucous, spirited note and ends in ominous terror.

The film dramatizes the struggles of a medieval doctor, Paracelsus, as he works to overcome scientific and medical misunderstanding, small-mindedness and backwardness in the battle against plague.  If the film had a propagandistic point, it presumably was to present Paracelsus as a glorified antecedent to Adolf Hitler though, in the doctor's rebellion against established bureaucratic authority, one could as easily come to a subversive point of view.  At any rate, the Nazi censors apparently did not see, or care to see, anything objectionable, and the film does end on an upbeat note extolling German nationalism.

Two of the greatest figures in German cinema worked on the film: G.W. Pabst directing and Werner Krauss acting the title role.  Nonetheless, the film is, overall, static and preachy.  It is decidedly inferior in

just about all respects to Ingmar Bergman's *The Seventh Seal*—which deals with similar subject matter—although sequential screenings of the two films would be a fascinating exercise.

The film can be obtained either with or without English subtitles.   See also ETERNAL CIRCLE.

## PAS DE DEUX.  14 min., 1968, b/w.**

*Rental $3.60 from Michigan, $5.50 from Kent State, $5.50 from Syracuse, $5.75 from Minnesota, $6.90 from Illinois, $7 from South Florida, $7 from Penn State, $7.50 from Em Gee, $8.25 from Indiana, $10 from USC, $10 from Kit Parker, $10 from Budget, $14 from Rochester, $15 from Viewfinders, $15 from California, $15 from Pyramid, $25 from LCA. Sale $170 from LCA.*
An extraordinarily beautiful film by Canadian filmmaker, Norman McLaren.

Two dancers were filmed in slow motion (half speed) performing choreography of a fairly conventional adagio to haunting panpipe music.  Dressed in white and back-lit to illuminate the outlines of their bodies, they moved through a black room.  The basic technique used throughout the film is the multiple superimposition of frames so that one sees not only where the dancer is now, but also where he or she was five, ten, or twenty frames ago.  If the dancer is at rest, only one image will appear since all the frames will show the same pose; if the dancer is moving, multiple images will be seen.  The technique is also used to allow the dancers to appear to meld into and then out of poses and to allow them to appear to be dancing with a reflection of themselves.

PAS DE DEUX

There is a distinct technical progression in the film as the use of the multiple exposures gets more complex, and through all the abstract camera tricks a flowing and, finally, sensuous effect is created.

Called, by some, "a true extension of the essence of dance through the medium of film." Winner of multiple awards.

The dancers are Margaret Mercier and Vincent Warren; the choreographer, Ludmilla Chiriaeff. McLaren discusses his method in the June 1970 issue of *Film News*. See also his BALLET ADAGIO.

## PAUL TAYLOR AND COMPANY: AN ARTIST AND HIS WORK. 33 min., 1968, color.*

*Rental $11.45 from Minnesota, $13.75 from Syracuse, $13.90 from Illinois, $14 from Penn State, $14.50 from Michigan, $30 from USC, $35 from Pyramid. Sale $375 from Pyramid.*

This attractive documentary on Taylor and his company includes excerpts from *Three Epitaphs*, *Lento*, *Agathe's Tale*, *Orbs*, *Aureole*, and *Piece Period*. Although far too brief, these bits do serve to illustrate the various sides of Taylor's work: the comic, the lyric, the grotesque. The company is shown rehearsing, fund raising, performing, demonstrating, relaxing. Directed by Ted Steeg.

Seen in action are Taylor, Bettie de Jong, Daniel Williams, Carolyn Adams, Daniel Wagoner, Jane Kosminsky, Eileen Cropley, Janet Aaron, Mollie Reinhart, Cliff Keuter, Senta Driver, John Nightingale. Adams and Williams perform major portions of the duet from *Lento*, now often performed separately and known simply as *Duet*. See also JUNCTION.

## PETER RABBIT AND THE TALES OF BEATRIX POTTER. 98 min., 1970, color. X*

*Had been available for rental from Films, Inc. but has been withdrawn.*

Members of the Royal Ballet, in animal masks and costumes, romp through several of these classic stories to choreography by Frederick Ashton (who also appears as Mrs. Tiggywinkle). A book has been written on this film and the process of making it: Rumer Godden, *The Tale of Tales: The Beatrix Potter Ballet* (London and N.Y.: Warne & Co., $17.50). For a review of the film by Arlene Croce, see *Ballet Review*, Vol. 3, No. 6.

## PETER TCHAIKOVSKY STORY. 30 min., 1959, color.

*Rental $10 from South Florida, $11 from Kentucky, $11.25 from Iowa, $11.50 from Southern Illinois, $11.55 from Illinois, $12.50 from Boston, $14 from Penn State, $20 from Association.*

A factually free-wheeling biography of the composer by Walt Disney and friends. Happens to contain, however, some glimpses of Ulanova in *Swan Lake* as well as four Bolshoi dancers in the cygnet dance, taken from the *Swan Lake* portion of the film, STARS OF THE RUSSIAN BALLET.

## PLISETSKAYA DANCES. 70 min., 1964, b/w.**

*Rental $21.50 from Illinois, $35 from Syracuse, $65 (higher for large audiences or where admission is charged) from Audio Brandon. Sale $655 from Audio Brandon.*

This documentary on one of the world's great ballerinas is one of the most popular dance films ever made. Plisetskaya (b. 1925) is seen in a number of substantial onstage excerpts. These include: 1) parts of the *Black Swan Pas de Deux* with Nikolai Fadeyechev; 2) the adagio from the *Sleeping Beauty Pas de Deux* with Fadeyechev following a rehearsal of it under Marina Semyonova's direction in which tricky camera work makes Plisetskaya's spins seem even faster than they already are; 3) the female variation for the same duet; 4) a solo from Chabukiani's *Laurencia* including her famous back-of-the-head kick; 5) silent movie acting from Leonid Yacobson's *Spartacus* (with Dmitri Begak); 6) a bit from Alexander Radunsky's *Little Humpbacked Horse* with Marius Liepa; 7) a solo from *Khovanchina*; 8) about three-eighths of the *Swan Lake* Act II adagio with Fadeyechev; 9) her effective version (not Fokine's) of *The Dying Swan*; 10) a solo from *Raymonda* Act III; 11) some moments from Lavrovksy's *Stone Flower* with Vasiliev; 12) lengthy excerpts from Lavrovsky's *Romeo and Juliet* with Yuri Zhdanov (except for a brief wedding sequence that gives us more Fadeyechev); 13) some *Walpurgisnacht* with Liepa; and 14) explosive sequences from *Don Quixote* with V. Tikhanov.

PLISETSKAYA DANCES

The narration is cloying, but bearable. For far more depth into Plisetskaya's personality, political position, and perspectives (including a description of her reactions while watching this film), see the profile of her in George Feifer, *Our Motherland* (Viking, 1973). See also Agnes de Mille's comments in *Dance Perspectives* No. 44, p. 49.

PROCESSION: CONTEMPORARY DIRECTIONS IN AMERICAN DANCE. 17 min., 1967, b/w.

*Rental $6.65 from Iowa, $6.70 from Illinois, $15 from California. Sale $150 from California.*

Ann Halprin and the Dancer's Workshop Company of San Francisco perform selections from *Procession*, a dance from their experimental repertory.

In this presentation of "total theater," the dancers interact with one another and with the elements of their stage environment (light, electronic sound, scaffolding, articles of clothing, and other props) as they seek to carry out a simple task: keep moving forward. Halprin explains her aesthetic position and comments on her group's approach to dance.

RADHA. 19 min., 1941, color.

*Rental $12 from Rochester.*

Ruth St. Denis with a framing corps of men (including Donald Saddler) were filmed performing this famous exotic work in the open air at Jacob's Pillow in Massachusetts in 1941. The filmmaker, Dwight Godwin, edited the film in 1972, coordinating the movements with the appropriate Edouard Lalo music. St. Denis was sixty-two when the film was made and no longer had the brilliance of movement and suppleness of body that the work requires for proper effect. However, Godwin has inserted still photographs from early performances between the sections of the dance and these help one considerably to appreciate the film and to visualize how *Radha* must have looked at its premiere in 1906. A film for specialists.

The performance is preceded by a six-minute introduction by Walter Terry. For St. Denis' own commentary on the premiere of *Radha*, see her autobiography *An Unfinished Life*, pp. 70-71.

RAINFOREST. 26 min., 1969, color.*

*Rental $12.50 from Illinois. Rental $30, sale $300 from Pennebaker.*

A film recording the first performance (in 1968 in Buffalo, NY) of this rather somber and mysterious work which features, as decor, the beautiful, helium-filled silver pillows designed by Andy Warhol.

Camera placements in the orchestra pit are less than ideal and much of the camera work is so close-in that, while the theatrical effect of the work is sub-

stantially preserved, the full shape of the choreography is blurred. There is also some introductory documentary material on the company, the choreographer, and composer-musician John Cage, and there is a brief interview in which Cunningham somehow fashions some enormously intelligent answers to some pretty shallow questions.

Featured dancers (in order of appearance) include Cunningham, Barbara Lloyd, Albert Reid, Gus Solomons, Jr., Carolyn Brown, and Sandra Neels. The electronic music (changed later) was by David Tudor.

F. RANDOLPH AND ASSOCIATES FILMS. 1300 Arch Street, Philadelphia, PA 19107; (215) 567-0505. A series of thirteen short color films on various ethnic dance styles. See also INTRODUCTION TO DUNCAN DANCES.

REACHING. 12 min., 1974, color.

*Rental $35, sale $140 from Steeg.*

Walter Nicks in a mostly-black elementary school in Wilmington, Delaware, as part of the Artists in Schools program.

RED DETACHMENT OF WOMEN. 100 min., color.*

*Rental $50 from US-China Friendship Assn., 41 Union Square West, NYC, or $100 from The Newsreel, 630 Natoma Street, San Francisco, CA 94103; (415) 621-6196.*

The Chinese Communist ballet.

RED SHOES. 133 min., 1948, color.*

*Rental $65 from Select, $67.50 from Budget, $75 from Audio Brandon, $85 from Twyman.*

The famous melodrama about a young dancer (Moira Shearer) and her problems. Leonide Massine appears prominently and impressively. Choreography mostly by Robert Helpmann, who also appears in the film.

REFLECTIONS ON CHOREOGRAPHY. 13 min., 1973, color.

*For rental contact Professor Allegra Fuller Snyder, Dept. of Dance, UCLA, Los Angeles, CA 90024.*

Marion Scott discusses her work, *Abyss*, and UCLA students perform it.

RHYTHMETRON. 40 min., 1973, color.

*Rental $16.35 from Northern Illinois, $16.50 from Kent State, $17.50 from Illinois, $18.65 from Michigan, $19.50 from Penn State, $21.50 from South Florida, $25 from USC, $35 from Syracuse. Rental $45, sale $570 from McGraw-Hill.*

A documentary on Arthur Mitchell and his all-black Dance Theatre of Harlem, first telecast on PBS in 1973 in a somewhat longer version. The film discusses Mitchell's decision, after the assassination of Martin Luther King, Jr. in 1968, largely to abandon his dancing career and devote himself to creating a ballet school in Harlem for the training of black talent. The company was formed two years later. Mitchell enthusiastically talks about his work and is seen teaching class and reflecting on his past.

The longest section of the film, apparently shot in a television studio, shows a spirited lecture-demonstration that takes place before an audience of entranced grade-school kids. Members of the company demonstrate while Mitchell explains the origins of the steps, often relating them to social dance steps like the "monkey" or the "penguin," and often comparing the dancer's training to that of the athlete. The discussion is quite basic, beginning with turnout and pliés, and is reasonably informative and engaging. It does not include much in the way of a demonstration of the more exciting pyrotechnic steps.

The film concludes with three examples of Mitchell's choreography, serviceable at best: sections from *Fête Noire*, *Biosfera*, and *Rhythmetron*. The filmed performances are weak and tentative, far below the young company's best effort and much below their present standards. Directed by Milton Fruchtman.

RISE OF LOUIS XIV. 100 min., 1966, color.*

*Rental $125 (higher for large audiences or where admission is charged) from Audio Brandon.*

Roberto Rossellini's exquisite reconstruction of the era, showing the meticulous social manners and forms through which Louis exuded his authority. Although not used in the film, dance and ballet spectacles were part of Louis' arsenal.

ROADS TO HELL. 22 min., 1948, b/w, silent. ?

*Rental probably $30 or more from Bouchard.*

Eleanor King in her solo dance work which was conceived as a suite of satires without music. The four parts are "Pride," "Sloth," "Envy," and "Wrath."

ROMEO AND JULIET BALLET. 126 min., 1966, color.**

*Rental $75 from Syracuse, $125 (higher for large audiences or where admission is charged) from Audio Brandon or from Association. (When ordering, be sure to specify the dance version; otherwise you may get Lawrence Harvey or Leslie Howard, instead of Rudolf Nureyev.)*

This beautiful film was made in 1966 by Paul Czinner in a specially designed studio. It features the original Royal Ballet cast headed by Rudolf Nureyev and Margot Fonteyn. The dancing is splendid, the sets and costumes (Nicholas Georgiadis) are splendid, the music (Serge Prokofiev) is splendid, the camera work is splendid. And most people will find Kenneth MacMillan's choreography acceptable at least. Also in the cast are David Blair, Desmond Doyle, and Julia Farron.

Rudolf Nureyev and the Royal Ballet in ROMEO AND JULIET BALLET

ROMEO AND JULIET (BALLET OF ROMEO AND JULIET). 96 min., 1954, color.

*Rental $150 (classroom $75) from Radim.*

Galina Ulanova, Yuri Zhdanov, and the Bolshoi Ballet in the Lavrovsky choreography, some filmed in a studio, some outdoors.

THE ROYAL BALLET. 132 min., 1959, color.**

*Available on 35mm and probably on 16mm from Schoenfeld.*

A splendid film featuring the performances of Margot Fonteyn and Michael Somes in three works filmed on stage in full production by Paul Czinner.

The film begins with sixteen minutes from Act II of *Swan Lake* with an active Benno (Bryan Ashbridge) in the adagio and with Antoinette Sibley as a cygnet. Then Fokine's complete *Firebird* with the sets and costumes of Natalia Gontcharova as designed for the 1926 Diaghilev version. Finally, Ashton's three-act ballet of 1958, *Ondine*, with Alexander Grant as Tirrenio.

RUSSIAN BALLERINA. See GREAT BALLERINA.

RUSSIAN BALLET AND FOLK DANCES. 10 min., 1944, b/w.*

*Rental $3.50 from Boston, $8.50 from Audio*

*Brandon. Sale $50 from Dance Films, $85 from Audio Brandon.*

A collection of four numbers: 1) Olga Lepeshinskaya in solo variations from Act I of *Don Quixote*; 2) Galina Ulanova and Konstantin Sergeyev in three-quarters of the *Swan Lake* Act II adagio, performed without corps; 3) some energetic, if brief, balalaika playing by Atai Obonbayev and two pupils; 4) an all-out effort by a group called "The Ukrainian Song and Dance Ensemble of the Don Bas Coal Miners." The first three are also included in BALLET CONCERT.

## RUTH ST. DENIS AND TED SHAWN. 30 min., 1958.**

*Rental $6.50 from Michigan, $7 from Minnesota, $7.50 ($15 in East) from Utah, $8.30 from Southern Illinois, $8.40 from Illinois, $11 from Penn State, $12 from UCLA, $14 from California. Sale from Films Inc.*

An excellent, revealing film on the dancers, filmed at Jacob's Pillow by NBC with commentary by Walter Terry.

Shawn is interviewed first and he quotes Nietzsche, discusses dance as a ministry, and patiently explains how dance becomes trivial if it is dominated by women. He then glowers and tumbles his way through his solo work, *Japanese Warrior*.

St. Denis is then interviewed by Shawn, who seems almost puppy-like in her presence. They reminisce and she performs two solos: the sensuous *Incense* and *White Nautch*. Telecast November 3, 1957 as part of NBC's "Wisdom" series.

## RUTH ST. DENIS BY BARIBAULT. 24 min., color.**

*Rental $19, sale $285 from Rochester.*

Five numbers by the famous dancer, unobtrusively filmed in beautiful color in the 1940s and early 1950s by her friend, Phillip Baribault, a professional Hollywood cameraman.

*Incense* from RUTH ST. DENIS BY BARIBAULT

Included are: 1) *White Jade*, showing the St. Denis skill at handling gowns and veils; 2) *Red and Gold Sari*, a flirtatious street dance; 3) *Gregorian Chant*, a somber religious expression in which St. Denis is accompanied by a male chorus; 4) *Tillers of the Soil*, a vignette about living off the land, with Ted Shawn—apparently the only film available showing the two performers dancing together; and 5) *Incense*, sensuous, religious, and ecstatic, featuring the famous arm ripple.

The sound, recorded live optically, leaves something to be desired and is quite poor on the *Red and Gold Sari* and *Tillers of the Soil* numbers. See also INCENSE.

## SADLER'S WELLS BALLERINA. 12 min., 1952, color.*

*Rental $5 from Michigan, $6.15 from Illinois, $8.50 from UCLA. Sale from International Film Foundation, 475 Fifth Avenue, NYC 10017.*

A pleasant and informative documentary by Julien Bryan on the daily life of the young dancer, Patricia Miller. Includes the last three minutes of John Cranko's 1949 ballet, *Beauty and the Beast*. Antony Tudor narrates.

## SADLER'S WELLS BALLET SCHOOL. 5 min., 1930s or 1940s, b/w.

*Rental $1.50 from Kentucky.*

Documentary on dance training at the school from first classes through graduation into the professional companies of Sadler's Wells and Covent Garden.

## SALOME. 35 min., 1922, b/w, silent.

*Rental $10 from South Florida, $12.50 from Kit Parker, $25 from Em Gee. Sale $120 from Em Gee, $150 from Kit Parker.*

Alla Nazimova in an Oscar Wilde-inspired spectacle. The highly stylized decor was executed by Natacha Rambova (Mrs. Rudolph Valentino) after Aubrey Beardsley drawings. Directed by Charles Bryant.

## SATIN SLIPPERS. 32 min., 1949, b/w.

*Rental $8.50 from USC, $13 from Audio Brandon. Sale $195 from Audio Brandon.*

On the rise of ballet in Australia. Performance, backstage, and rehearsal scenes. (A longer version, 51 min., is also available from Audio Brandon.)

## SCAPE-MATES. 28 min., 1972, color.*

*Rental $40 from FMC.*

A film by Ed Emshwiller, originally done for television, featuring two dancers (Sarah Shelton and Emery Hermans) in a computer-animated environment.

## SCENES FROM B. ASAFYEV'S BALLET THE FLAMES OF PARIS. 22 min., 1953, b/w.*

*Rental $12.50 from Illinois.*
A non-stop romp through the French revolution, led by Chabukiani and Gottlieb. See also STARS OF THE RUSSIAN BALLET.

## SCENES FROM THE BALLET OF FOUNTAIN OF BAKHCHISARAI. 27 min., 1953, b/w.**

*Rental $13 from Illinois.*
Compressed version of the ballet, beautifully done. Features Galina Ulanova as Maria, Maya Plisetskaya as the Khan's favorite, Pyotr Gusev as the Khan, and Yuri Zhdanov as the Polish nobleman. See also STARS OF THE RUSSIAN BALLET.

## SCHOOL OF AMERICAN BALLET. 43 min., 1973, b/w.*

*Rental $25, sale $250 from Virginia Brooks, 460 Riverside Drive, NYC 10027; (212) 222-9887 (evenings mainly).*
Systematically this valuable film surveys the training at the school from beginning classes through a graduation workshop performance at the Juilliard Theatre. In between there are views of pointe, variations, men's, and adagio classes, and of a workshop rehearsal directed by Alexandra Danilova in which George Balanchine is seen tinkering with some of the choreography from the first act of *Swan Lake*.

The film makes no effort to belabor or exploit any physical or psychological stresses some of the students may undergo. It is content, simply and unpretentiously, to document the dedication and plain hard work that go into the training of a professional ballet dancer.

A narration, spoken by one of the students, explains how the school is organized and how the school organizes its students' lives. The late Eugenie Ouroussow appears briefly and discusses the school's origins in 1934. Among the teachers seen in action are (besides Danilova) Felia Doubrovska, Muriel Stuart, Helene Dudin, Antonia Tumkovsky, Elise Reiman, and Stanley Williams. Helgi Tomasson, from New York City Ballet, is seen guest-teaching an adagio class.

The footage was shot in 1972, a year in which the school's prize pupil was Fernando Bujones, later to win a gold medal in the Varna competition and now a principal dancer with American Ballet Theatre. This unusually promising student is shown extensively in class and rehearsal.

## SEAFALL. 11 min., 1969, color.*

*Rental $20, sale $135 from Schoenfeld.*
Intensely romantic and poetic, suggested by Edgar Allan Poe's poem, "Annabel Lee." The dancers are Lisa Bradley and Michael Uthoff. Stills and a discussion can be found in *DM*, August 1970. Filmed by Gardner Compton. Music attributed to Albinoni.

## SERAPHIC DIALOGUE. 25 min., 1969, color.**

*Rental $10.75 from Minnesota, $11.60 from Illinois, $20 from Budget, $25 from Pyramid. Sale $325 from Pyramid.*
Martha Graham's version of the story of Joan of Arc, choreographed in 1955. At the moment of her exaltation, Joan looks back over her life as a young girl, as a warrior, and as a martyr, and then is taken into the arms of the Saints. Her doubts, her trials, her relationship with St. Michael are explored.

SERAPHIC DIALOGUE (not the film cast)

Joan is danced by Mary Hinkson, St. Michael by Bertram Ross, Joan as a young girl by Patricia Birch, Joan as a warrior by Helen McGehee, Joan as a martyr by Noemi Lapzeson, St. Catherine by Phyllis Gutelius, St. Margaret by Takako Asakawa. The beautiful set is by Isamu Noguchi. Music by Norman Dello Joio. Adapted for camera by John Butler. Direction by Dave Wilson. The color is somewhat faded in quality.

THE SHAKERS. 15 min., 1940, b/w, silent.?*

*Rental $40 from Bouchard.*

Thomas Bouchard's silent film interpretation of the Doris Humphrey work set in a suggestion of a Shaker meeting house, featuring as dancers Humphrey, Charles Weidman, and José Limón. The film is gimmicky, but the performances are powerful.

An illustrated monograph on "The Dance in Shaker Ritual" appears in *Dance Index*, April 1942. For comments on Bouchard, see Margaret Lloyd, *Borzoi Book of Modern Dance*, pp. 350-351. There are also two documentary films on the Shaker sect, called "The Shakers" and "Shakers in America," available for rental at various places, including Illinois.

THE SHAKERS. 9 min., 1967, b/w.

*Rental $5 from Illinois, $8 from Ohio State. Sale $60 from Ohio State.*

Doris Humphrey's dance composition has been reconstructed from Labanotation by Janet Wynn Descutner and is performed by the University Dance Group of Ohio State University. Camera work gives an idea of what the work looks like on stage, but overactive directing often leaves much happening off-camera. Can instructively be compared to the Bouchard version above, see p. 12.

SHAPE (Murray Louis). See DANCE AS AN ART FORM.

SHE AND MOON DANCES. 14 min., 1940s, silent.?

*Rental probably from Bouchard.*

Excerpts from two works by Eleanor King. Two of the three sections ("The Mothers Create" and "The Mothers Possess") of the bitingly satiric 1948 dance work, *She*, occupy the first eight minutes of the film. The last six minutes present moments from King's eerie 1944 solo, *Moon Dances*. For a valuable discussion, see Margaret Lloyd, *Borzoi Book of Modern Dance*, pp. 293-294.

SLEEPING BEAUTY. 92 min., 1964, color, cinemascope (special anamorphic lens required for projector—see p. 6).**

*Rental $75 from Swank.*

A beautiful, nearly full-length rendering of the Petipa classic featuring the Kirov Ballet and some of its greatest dancers.

This film preserves the extraordinary performances of Alla Sizova as Aurora and the late Yuri Solovyov as the Prince. Under the guidance of Kirov artistic director Konstantin Sergeyev, the performance space has been tastefully and fairly imaginatively expanded from the theater onto a movie sound stage, keeping,

it appears, some of the sets and many of the costumes of the Kirov stage production. (The color quality is only adequate, however.) The camera work is generally quiet, sensitive, and unobtrusive, although there are a few occasional shifts of perspective that seem unnecessary and abrupt. In spots, the uniqueness of the film medium is sensibly used to advantage, as when the Wicked Fairy is made to vanish with an effectiveness impossible on the stage. But the ballet is about dancing and the film is mostly content to acknowledge that fact.

The Russian producers were apparently determined to keep the film within the bounds of a single sitting without intermission—ninety minutes. To do this they have cut the last act (known independently as *Aurora's Wedding*) to fifteen minutes. Left out completely is Petipa's sparkling "Precious Stones" quartet, and all that is included of the show-stopping *Bluebird Pas de Deux* is the adagio. And, since the Bluebird is Valery Panov and his partner is Natalia Makarova, both in excellent form in what was then their natural setting before their separate and highly publicized defections to the West, that is quite a loss.

But if we see Makarova and Panov only fleetingly, we are supplied with an extended in-depth display of Sizova and Solovyov, both in their mid-twenties when the film was made. Sizova's Aurora is justly famous. She is a bit cold on the screen but her authority in the role, her firm balances, improbable extensions and elevation are impressive indeed. And, like ex-Kirov dancer Mikhail Baryshnikov, Solovyov had an ability to propel himself deftly into space without apparent preparation and could dish out seemingly effortless triple tours en l'air.

Also in the cast is Natalia Dudinskaya, on pointe, as Carabosse, the "Wicked Fairy." She was in her early fifties when the film was made but seems to have lost little of her legendary control and forcefulness, although the additional choreography supplied for her by Sergeyev (her husband) lacks distinction. She is a first-rate actress and tends to dominate the screen whenever she is on it. (Much of the acting by the rest of the cast is pretty perfunctory.) The Lilac Fairy is danced effectively, though less than radiantly, by Irina Bazhenova. Among her ancillary fairies is Kaleria Fedicheva, like Panov and Makarova, a recent self-exile to the West. The other fairies are E. Minchenok, T. Korneyeva, L. Kovalyova, and N. Sakhnovskaya. The Kirov corps, looking good but less than stunning, is displayed in the garland waltz and the vision scene.

In showing the film there is a convenient place for an intermission should you have an alert projectionist. At the end of Act I, after the Princess falls into her 100-year sleep, the camera freezes for a few seconds on a still view of her castle, and the music stops. A break here would conveniently divide the film into one fifty-minute and one forty-two-minute segment. This arrangement would also make it possible to show the film with a single projector.

The film comes with about three minutes of music with no picture both at the beginning and at the end which can be used as prologue and as exit music for an audience. Surrounding the opening credits there is footage of the good and bad fairies dancing in their separate spheres. A short portion of this is wildly out of sync and it gives an audience an unpleasant moment of fear that the whole film will be that way (it is not). A knowledgeable audience should probably be forewarned about the cuts in the Bluebird duet to forestall groans and anguish when that part of the film comes up. An interesting film to program with this one might be BAYADERKA, which features Dudinskaya in younger days.

In *Dance Perspectives* No. 49, Soviet scholar Vera Krasovskaya analyzes Petipa's *Sleeping Beauty* with many pictures from the original production of 1890. Olga Maynard engagingly traces the history of various productions of the ballet in a portfolio distributed by *DM*. And Petipa's complete scenario for the ballet is reprinted in the book, *Making a Ballet*, by Clement Crisp and Mary Clarke.

## SOVIET ARMY SONG AND DANCE ENSEMBLE.

*Presently available only in 35mm, from Celebrity. Rental from $500 to $750 for one showing, but a percentage-of-gross arrangement can be made. There is also an $18 handling and inspection charge.*

## SPACE (Murray Louis). See DANCE AS AN ART FORM.

## SPANISH FIESTA (CAPRICCIO ESPAGNOL). 20 min., 1941, color.

*Rental $9 from Illinois, $20 (members only) from Dance Films. Sale $200 from Dance Films.*

Leonide Massine's ballet in a Warner Brother production. Features Massine, Tamara Toumanova, Alexandra Danilova, Frederic Franklin, Andre Eglevsky, and the Ballet Russe de Monte Carlo. The manic direction is by Jean Negulesco.

## SPIRIT OF THE DANCE (LE SPECTRE DE LA DANSE). 22 min., 1965, b/w.*

*Rental $20, sale $150 from Radim.*

In class, rehearsal, and performance, the professional life of a dancer, Nina Vyroubova of the Paris Opéra, is unobtrusively explored. In one sequence, the ballerina learns the role of *Giselle* from a film, aided by Serge Lifar.

## SPRING NIGHT. 10 min., 1935, b/w.*

*Rental $6 from Budget, $13 from Ivy Film, 165 W. 46 Street, NYC 10036.*

Engaging, rather exotic fantasy duet choreographed in Hollywood by David Lichine for himself and the fifteen-year-old Nana Gollner.

This short, subtitled "A ballet in dramatic form," was produced by Adolf Zukor and was one of Hollywood's fleeting and self-conscious efforts to do "culture." A young servant girl, dreamily romantic, wanders through a garden past a statue of a reclining faun. She falls into a fantasy. She sees herself in an abbreviated dress and the faun (Lichine) comes to life and playfully chases her through the forest. He catches her and, as she is about to give in to his embrace, her eyes closed, her father interrupts the reverie. As she is led home, the faun statue is seen to have a tear in its eye.

Suggestive in some ways of Nijinsky's *Afternoon of a Faun* and Fokine's *Spectre of the Rose*, this gently erotic film would make an attractive, rather exotic, addition to many film programs. Lichine, who provided the choreography, at the time was a member of the de Basil Ballet Russe and Gollner was to become a leading dancer with Ballet Theatre.

## SQUAREGAME. 27 min., 1978, b/w, videotape.

*Rental on videotape $50 from Cunningham Dance Foundation.*

A video recording by Charles Atlas of the 1976 Merce Cunningham work.

## STARS OF THE RUSSIAN BALLET. 80 min., 1953, b/w.*

*Rental $40 (higher for large audiences or where admission is charged) from Audio Brandon. Sale from Audio Brandon.*

Three compressed ballets, each twenty to thirty minutes in length: 1) *Swan Lake* with Ulanova as the white swan, Dudinskaya as the black swan, and K. Sergeyev as the prince. Cartoons are used to effect the swan transformations; 2) *The Fountain of Bakhchisarai*, a highly effective version of the ballet to Alexander Pushkin's poem, with Ulanova as Maria, Plisetskaya as the Khan's favorite, Gusev as the Khan, and Zhdanov as the Polish noblemen; 3) *The Flames of Paris*, a non-stop romp through the French Revolution, led by Chabukiani and Gottlieb.

The three ballets are also available separately. See the listings STARS OF THE RUSSIAN BALLET—SWAN LAKE, SCENES FROM THE BALLET OF FOUNTAIN OF BAKHCHISARAI, and SCENES FROM B. ASAFYEV'S BALLET THE FLAMES OF PARIS.

STARS OF THE RUSSIAN BALLET—SWAN LAKE.
33 min., 1953, b/w.

*Rental $14 from Illinois.*

Compressed version of the ballet with Galina
Ulanova as the white swan, Natalia Dudinskaya as the
black swan, and Konstantin Sergeyev as the prince.
Cartoons are used to effect the swan transformations.
See also STARS OF THE RUSSIAN BALLET.

STEPS OF THE BALLET.   25 min., 1948, b/w.

*Rental $4 from Kentucky, $5.75 from Boston,
$5.95 from Minnesota, $7.30 from Illinois, $7.50
($15 in East) from Utah, $8.75 from Indiana, $9.50
from UCLA, $25 from Radim.  Sale $225 from
Radim.*

Robert Helpmann talks about how a ballet is
constructed by the choreographer (Andrée Howard),
composer, and artist.  The dancers include Alexander
Grant, Elaine Fifield, Michael Boulton, Gerd Larsen,
and Gordon Hamilton.  Directed by Muir Mathieson.

STORY. 20 min., 1964, b/w.

*Rental $50 from Cunningham Dance Foundation.
Also available for purchase.*

Merce Cunningham's indeterminate work filmed in
Finland during a tour.  Decor by Robert Rauschenberg.

STRAVINSKY. 52 min., 1966, b/w.*

*Rental $19 from Rochester.*

A documentary by CBS News on the famous composer who was then eighty-three years old.  Included
is a fascinating eight-minute sequence in which
Stravinsky revisits the Théâtre des Champs-Elysées in
Paris where Nijinsky's *Sacre du Printemps* was pre-
miered in 1913.  He discusses the tumultuous circumstances of that night, shows where he was sitting, and
retraces his steps. (Note: This segment is not included
in the version of this program—which has been
reduced to "classroom length"—distributed by
Carousel Films.)

Also shown is a passage from a contemporary version of the ballet, distinctly unlike the original,
danced by Elizabeth Jaron and the Warsaw Opera
Ballet.  There is also a brief segment in which Stravinsky visits George Balanchine in New York and sees
Suzanne Farrell (soon to appear in Balanchine's ballet
to Stravinsky's *Variations*) put through some paces.

In the rest of the film the composer is shown con-
ducting *Firebird Suite* in Poland, recording *Ebony
Concerto* with Benny Goodman, listening to a performance of *Symphony of Psalms* with Pope Paul,
sketching and being sketched by Alberto Giacometti,

and talking with students in Texas.  He discusses his
music ("there are pages of *Sacre* which I like and I
find them interesting today and there are tens of
pages to which I am absolutely indifferent today—
this means that I change"), seriality, critics, religion
("I believe because it is absurd"), Mozart, Richard
Strauss, his need for rules in music, mood ("mood is
for girls"), and expression in music ("Can express
nothing.  That is my conviction—can express itself
only.").

STUDY IN CHOREOGRAPHY FOR CAMERA.  4
min., 1940s, b/w, silent.

*Rental $4.60 from Minnesota, $5.75 from Indiana,
$15 from Grove.  Sale at least $85 from Grove.*

A classic experimental dance film by Maya Deren
featuring dancer Talley Beatty.

SUE'S LEG:  REMEMBERING THE THIRTIES.  59
min., 1976, color.**

*Rental $20.75, sale $550 from Indiana.*

A half-hour documentary on dance styles and fads
of the 1930s coupled with a complete performance of
Twyla Tharp's *Sue's Leg*, a brilliant dance work
choreographed in 1974 and set to tunes played by
Fats Waller.  Dancing in the work are Tharp, Rose-
Marie Wright, Kenneth Rinker, and Tom Rawe.

Twyla Tharp in SUE'S LEG

The connected documentary is a breezy, engaging overview of the 1930s: flagpole dancing, the tap craze, marathon dances, etc. It attempts in part to show the era to which Tharp's dance work relates, though some of the specific comparisons seem rather strained. It relies heavily on newsreel footage and this inevitably leads to an emphasis on the kitsch and the trendy.

Shown before *Sue's Leg* as intended, the *Remembering the Thirties* documentary has something of a deadening effect on the dance work, and may be even something of a trivializing one. After a half hour of a rapid sampling of flamboyant and outrageous dance capers, it is somewhat difficult suddenly to have to concentrate on extended choreography. Also the felicities of popular 1930s music may begin to wear a bit thin before Tharp's dancers take over.

Therefore, in showing this film to an audience, it might be wise either to show the two parts on separate occasions or else to show them in reverse order. (The two sections come on separate reels.)

The program is part of the PBS "Dance in America" series and is capably directed by Merrill Brockway. The quality of the transfer from videotape is rather good, though a little dark in spots.

## SUGAR PLUM FAIRY VARIATION FROM THE BALLET "THE NUTCRACKER." 3 min., 1941, b/w.

*Rental (members only) $5, sale $50 from Dance Films.*
Alicia Markova performs, outdoors, at Jacob's Pillow. Sound added later.

## SURE, I CAN DANCE. 25 min., color.

*Rental $35, sale $350 from Radim.*
Featuring the Ririe-Woodbury Dance Company as Artists in the Schools.

## SWAN LAKE. 10 min., 1930s, b/w.

*Rental $3.50 from Boston, $5 from Indiana.*
Marina Semyonova and corps in some sort of choreography to music from Act II of Swan Lake. Also available on BALLET CONCERT.

## SWAN LAKE. 23 min., 1949, b/w.

*Rental $7.50 ($15 in East) from Utah, $17.50 from Audio Brandon.*
A very poor version in an outdoor setting by de Basil's Original Ballet Russe.

## SWAN LAKE. 81 min., 1959, color. ?

*A more-or-less full-length version, featuring Plisetskaya and Fadeyechev, apparently no longer available on 16mm. A 35mm print may be available for rental for $100 through Clyde Norton, Theatrical Sales, Audio Brandon.*

## SWAN LAKE.

*Presently available only in 35mm, in color, with stereo sound, from Celebrity. Rentals are $500 to $750 for one showing, but a percentage-of-gross arrangement can be made. There is also an $18 handling and inspection charge.*
A recent Kirov film production of the complete work featuring Yelena Yevteyeva and John Markovsky with Valery Panov as the Jester. For David Vaughan's review, see *Ballet Review*, Vol. 4, No. 1.

## SWEDEN: FIRE AND ICE. 52 min., 1964, b/w.**

*Rental $13 from Illinois, $14 (Miss Julie ballet only) from Rochester, $16 from Penn State. Rental $15, sale $260 from Modern Mass Media, 315 Springfield Avenue, Summit, NJ 07901.*
On thirty-five minutes of this film is a complete performance of Birgit Cullberg's 1950 ballet interpretation of the Strindberg play, *Miss Julie*, given an excellent performance by members of the Royal Swedish Ballet including Wiweka Ljung as Miss Julie, Conny Borg as Jean, and Catharina Ericsson as Jean's fiancée, Kristin.

In this version, originally designed for television, the work has been brilliantly arranged by the choreographer to use a single fixed camera position for each of the four scenes, with the action staged to move within the camera's field of view. Cullberg discusses the work in *Dance Perspectives* No. 29 and her television approach in an essay in Walter Sorell, *The Dance Has Many Faces*.

On the rest of the film are Bellman and Taube songs, sung in English by William Clouser, and Dag Hammarskjold writings read by the program's host, Max Von Sydow.

## LES SYLPHIDES. 4 min., 1952, b/w.

*Rental $7.50 from Audio Brandon.*
Ulanova and Preobrazhenski in the waltz pas de deux, slightly cut. Also available on CONCERT OF STARS.

## TALES OF HOFFMANN. 118 min., 1951, color.*

*Rental $37.50 from Select, $40 from Budget, $45 from Kit Parker, $65 from Audio Brandon, $65 from Association, $75 from Twyman.*

A lavish version of the Offenbach opera, written, produced, and directed by Michael Powell and Emeric Pressburger. Somewhat stronger on imagination than on taste.

A considerable amount of dance is used, particularly in the first two tales. The choreography is by Frederick Ashton, and it is danced splendidly by Moira Shearer and Ludmilla Tcherina with character roles interpreted stunningly by Ashton, Robert Helpmann, and, especially, Leonide Massine. Robert Rounseville (as Hoffmann) is one of the few singers to appear in the film, and he often seems out of place. Sir Thomas Beecham conducts. For a discussion, see David Vaughan, *Frederick Ashton and His Ballets*.

TALES OF THE VIENNA WOODS. 9 min., 1949, b/w.

*Rental $4.50 from Kent State, $5 from Illinois.*
Members of the ballet at the Salzburg Festival dance to the Johann Strauss music performed by the Vienna Philharmonic Orchestra.

TARANTOS. 81 min., 1963, color.

*Rental $75 (higher for large audiences or where admission is charged) from Audio Brandon.*
A Spanish gypsy version of *Romeo and Juliet* told, in part, through dance.

THIS IS "THE PLACE." 35 min., color.

*Rental $17 from Illinois. Sale $480 from Dance Centre of London, 936 N. Michigan Avenue, Chicago, IL 60611; (312) 649-0525.*
London's "The Place" is the home and the school of the London Contemporary Dance Theater. This documentary, narrated by a female student, shows the viewer around to classes, rehearsals, demonstrations, choreographic sessions, performances.

Students take both traditional ballet and "modern ballet" at the school. Classes in the latter are based on Martha Graham technique which is somehow explained without the use of the word "contraction."

The film, written, produced, and directed by Peter Selby, does give an idea of what the school and the company are about. There are a number of (uncredited) dance excerpts from the company's mostly member-choreographed repertory. (At one point the dancers are shown in the costumes for Graham's *Diversion of Angels*, but the work itself is not shown.) The camera work on the dance sequences is often too close and overactive.

THREE BY GRAHAM. 1969, color.**

The Martha Graham Company performs COR-TEGE OF EAGLES, ACROBATS OF GOD, and

SERAPHIC DIALOGUE. Performance quality is extraordinary. All three films are available from Minnesota, Illinois, Budget, and Pyramid. For more information, see entries for the individual dance compositions.

THREE DANCES 1964. 17 min., 1964, b/w.

*Rental $20, sale $200 from East End.*
*Public* explores the "dance" made by visitors to the Museum of Modern Art's sculpture garden. *Party* uses superimposed images to cover a social dance party of artists and dancers in an underlit gym (shown are Judith Dunn, Alex Hay, Robert Rauschenberg, Debbie Hay, Steve Paxton). *Private* is a solo in a loft (Judith Dunn) viewed by the distance-exaggerating wide-angle lens. Photography by Gene Friedman.

THREE EPITAPHS. 6 min., 1966, b/w. X*

*Information from Paul Taylor Dance Company, 550 Broadway, NYC 10012.*
Paul Taylor's quirky dance work with costumes by Robert Rauschenberg, capably filmed in West Germany. Not presently available.

TIME (Murray Louis). See DANCE AS AN ART FORM.

A TIME TO DANCE. 29 min., 1960, b/w.*

*Rental $9.50, sale $125 from Indiana.*
A discussion of the major dance forms of ballet, modern dance, and ethnic. Besides various clips, the film includes Spanish dance performed by the Ximenez-Vargas Ballet Espagnol, Melissa Hayden and Jacques d'Amboise in the version of George Balanchine's *Nutcracker Pas de Deux* (Sugar Plum Fairy) that was being done at that time, and Daniel Nagrin in his zoot-suit solo, *Strange Hero*. Part of Martha Myers' "A Time to Dance" series.

TONIGHT WE SING. 109 min., 1953, color.

*Rental $40 from Films Inc.*
A Hollywood feature that purports to be the biography of Sol Hurok. Tamara Toumanova, Hollywood's perennial ballerina, plays the role of Anna Pavlova and appears in a *Dying Swan*, the female variation (plus a whole bunch of fouettés) from the *Don Quixote Pas de Deux*, a moment from the *Dragonfly* solo, and a romp with chorus choreographed by David Lichine.

TOTEM. 16 min., 1963, color.*

*Rental $8.80 from Iowa, $9.55 from Michigan, $12.50 from Penn State, $20 from FMC. Sale probably from Grove.*

A reasonably engaging film interpretation by Ed Emshwiller of a dance work by Alwin Nikolais. Murray Louis and Gladys Bailin are featured dancers.

## TOUR EN L'AIR. 50 min., 1974, color.

*Rental $20.50 from Illinois, $22.30 from Michigan, $37 from California. Rental also from Syracuse. Rental $35, sale $595 from Eccentric Circle, Box 4085, Greenville, CT.*

An attractive documentary on David and Anna-Marie Holmes, the Canadian dancers who appear on Norman McLaren's beautiful BALLET ADAGIO dancing a slow motion version of the show-stopping lyric duet *Spring Water*.

They are seen performing, rehearsing, relaxing, teaching, and arranging their business affairs as international guest stars. The film is especially interesting if shown after BALLET ADAGIO to give some insight into the sweat, uncertainty, exhaustion, strain, and pain that are so much a part of the ballet dancer's ethereal and seemingly effortless art.

David and Anna-Marie Holmes are, as the film observes, partners in a triple sense: business associates, husband and wife, and companions in dance. The film, directed by Grant Munro of the National Film Board of Canada, follows them around the world to Germany, Cuba, London, Canada, Portugal, and the United States on their performance, teaching, and business schedule. There is footage of the *Spring Water* duet on stage, with the original music and the usual "Grecian" costumes. There is also a section of the *Don Quixote Pas de Deux* danced in Cuba by Alicia Alonso and Azari Plisetski. The film concludes in a Montreal studio where David pushes Anna-Marie (and himself) through some brutal rehearsals for the BALLET ADAGIO film.

## TRIADISCHE BALLETT (TRIADIC BALLET). 32 min., late 1960s, color.**

*Rental free from Modern Talking Picture Service.*

A recent reconstruction of Oskar Schlemmer's 1922 ballet under the direction of Hannes Winkler (who is also one of the three dancers) with music by Erich Ferstl. Schlemmer's widow served as artistic advisor.

For commentary and costume sketches, see Lincoln Kirstein, *Movement and Metaphor*, pp. 214-217, *Dance Perspectives* No. 41, and Walter Gropius (ed.), *The Theatre of the Bauhaus*. See also MENSCH UND KUNSTFIGUR.

## TRICK DANCE FILM. 11 min., 1926, b/w., silent.

*Rental $10 from Audio Brandon.*

Features "Mme. Eleanor and the Belcher Ballet Company" and uses trick photographic devices, some

of which anticipate Busby Berkeley's geometrics or McLaren's PAS DE DEUX.

## TRIKFILM NO. 1. 1 min., color. X

*No longer available apparently.*

An animated film by George Griffin of a woman dancing with three images superimposed.

## USA: DANCE.**

A series of films of high quality produced in the mid-1960s by Jac Venza. Listed under "DANCE:" above.

## VARIATIONS AND CONCLUSION OF NEW DANCE—RECORD FILM. 7 min., 1978, color.*

*Rental $10, sale $150 from Rochester.*

The exultant concluding section of Doris Humphrey's modern dance classic of affirmation, choreographed in 1935. This popular section was often performed separately.

This is a *record film* (single, fixed camera), of the reconstruction (from Labanotation) danced by the professional Repertory Company at the 1972 American Dance Festival at Connecticut College. Music by Wallingford Riegger. For a film of the complete work, see NEW DANCE. For suggestions about showing this film, see p. 9.

## VARIATIONS V. 50 min., 1965, b/w. ?*

*Rental and sale possibly from Cunningham Dance Foundation.*

An excellent version of the rather zany Merce Cunningham work, made for German television. Music by John Cage, decor by Stan Van Der Beek.

## THE VERY EYE OF NIGHT. 14 min., 1958, b/w.

*Rental $35, sale at least $165 from Grove.*

An experimental dance film by Maya Deren. It is filmed in negative and features dancers who seem to drift among the stars. Music by Teijo Ito. Made in collaboration with Metropolitan Opera Ballet students under the direction of Antony Tudor.

The dancers are Richard Sandlifer, Don Freisinger, Patricia Ferrier, Bud Bready, Ginaro Gomez, Barbara Levin, Richard Englund, Rosemary Williams, Philip Salem.

## A VIDEO EVENT, PART 1 and PART 2. 30 min. each, 1974, color, videotape.**

*For purchase on videotape only. See CAMERA THREE.*

Two fine half-hour programs from CBS' *Camera Three* series featuring Merce Cunningham and dance company in excerpts from the repertory, each interestingly introduced by Cunningham.

The first program includes portions of *Winterbranch* (1964), Cunningham's remarkable opening solo from *Second Hand* (1970), six overdirected minutes from the agitated *Sounddance* (1974), and sequences from *TV Rerun* (1972). The second program (probably the better of the two) includes four portions of *Changing Steps* (1973) done simultaneously on a split screen, two parts of *Landrover* (1972) including an exquisite duet for Susana Hayman-Chaffey and Charles Moulton, and two witty sections from *Signals* (1970). Directed by Merrill Brockway. For more commentary see *DM*, July 1975.

VIDEO EXCHANGE. 151 Banks Street, NYC 10014; (212) 691-5035. ?

An organization that has been dedicated to recording and distributing dance materials on videotape.

The organization may have available recordings of works by Phyllis Lamhut, Meredith Monk, William Dunas, Sukanya, Dan Wagoner, June Lewis, Ze'eva Cohen, Rudy Perez, Arthur Bauman, Frances Alenikoff, Judith Dunn, Gus Solomons, Jr., Linda Tarnay, Kei Takei, Alice Condodina, Barbara Roan, Jeff Duncan, Deborah Jowitt, Vija Vetra, Edith Stephen, Margaret Beals, Emiko and Yasuko Tokunaga, Tina Croll, Sally Bowden, Carolyn Lord, Laura Dean, Jennifer Muller, Mary Fulkerson, and others.

WALKAROUND TIME.   48 min., 1973, color.**

*Rental $30 from FMC, $36 from Rochester. Sale $525 from Cunningham Dance Foundation.*

A fine film (though the work itself may be difficult for some audiences) by Charles Atlas of the wry, understated, ambling dance by Merce Cunningham. The stunning decor is by Jasper Johns—a segmentation of Marcel Duchamp's "Large Glass" onto a set of large translucent vinyl boxes.

The choreography is also, in part, an homage to Duchamp. There are dance characteristics which suggest elements of the "Large Glass": the chocolate grinder, the water wheel, the hovering bride (in a solo for Carolyn Brown). The work includes an "intermission" in which the dancers lounge around the stage in natural "readymade" poses. There are also references to *Relâche*, a ballet with which Duchamp was associated in 1924.

In addition there is a choreographic theme of progressing (of walking) across the proscenium space from one side to the other. The sparest expression of this is given to Meg Harper (at one point she simply walks across the stage), while the idea is developed to its most complex in a beautiful duet for Harper and Douglas Dunn in which they progress across the stage, though the progress is halted and temporarily reversed at times, tortured almost, as they lean and pull against each other. There are many applications of the idea: the dancers travel across in leaps, in hops, in fluttering kicks; Cunningham's jogging that sets each half of the work in motion; Dunn begins a solo on the left, poses, and is carried by several dancers to the other side where, replaced, he continues the solo which includes many aspects, stylized or not, of walking (including a suggestion of the Rodin sculpture, "Walking Man"). But the most extraordinary expression comes near the end of the work in a contrast between a minimum and a maximum walk: as Cunningham inches himself across the stage moving only his feet, Sandra Neels is given a slow motion, expansive run, choreographed down to the fingertip.

Atlas has filmed the work with quiet integrity. The film makes sensible how the work looked on stage and how the choreography shaped itself in the space. Even where one cannot see everything at once, the film almost always lets the viewer know where (and if) things are happening. Of course in the case of *Walkaround Time* the decor sometimes obscures some of the choreography from some of the audience, but one always knows where things are happening even if they cannot be made out completely and it is this feeling that is kept on the film. Toward the end, Atlas provides one of the most beautiful moments in all dance films: instead of following Sandra Neels in her exquisite slow motion run, Atlas fixes the camera on one spot, allowing her slowly to progress across its field of view from frame edge to frame edge—a kind of camera-eye perspective of the basic movement idea Cunningham is exploring in the dance work.

There are some bad moments early in the film—some jiggly camera work, some overly-close shots—and at times the camera seems a bit too distant, but these prove to be minor problems.

Among the values of this film is that it preserves the performances of some extraordinary Cunningham dancers no longer with the company. There is Valda Setterfield at her brightest and wittiest, the beautifully controlled Sandra Neels and Susana Hayman-Chaffey, the forceful Douglas Dunn, and Carolyn Brown, who can make an event of cosmic proportions out of simply standing still. Also on the film are Cunningham, Meg Harper, Chase Robinson, Chris Komar, and Ulysses Dove.

In creating the film, Atlas had originally intended a special mode of projection. The first section and the "intermission" would be projected in the usual way, but the second section would be shown in two views: two separate reels shown simultaneously by two interlocked projectors on a double-width screen. It takes special equipment to do this, but if you are interested in showing the film this way, contact the Cunningham Dance Foundation for information.

For further commentary see the article (inadvertently published in jumbled order) in *DM*, June 1977. See also ENTR'ACTE.

## WASH. 11 min., 1971, color.

*Rental $20, sale $165 from Radim.*
Billed as "a dance 'happening' on film," features the Ririe-Woodbury Dance Company and optical effects. Film by Judith and Stanley Hallet; produced by Joan Woodbury.

## WATCHING BALLET. 35 min., 1965, b/w.

*Rental $8.50 from Audio Brandon, $9 from Syracuse, $10 ($8 in New York State) from Association. Sale $165 from Association or Audio Brandon.*
A rather ingenuous lecture-demonstration by Jacques d'Amboise and Allegra Kent with two students, Colleen Neary and Paul Mejia.

The dance excerpts, all with choreography by George Balanchine, include: a female solo from *Gounod Symphony*, a fairly extensive section from the adagio of the *Nutcracker Pas de Deux*, a brief sequence from *Four Temperaments* featuring supported grand jetés, the male variation from the *Tchaikovsky Pas de Deux* rearranged for two men, part of the coda from *Pas de Dix*, a moment from the "Liberty Bell" duet in *Stars and Stripes*, the last part of the *Swan Lake* adagio, a pose from *Episodes*, and a complete duet from the divertissement from *Midsummer Night's Dream*.

## WESTBETH. 33 min., 1975, b/w.*

*Rental $15 from Rochester. Rental $40, sale $175 (on film or videotape) from Cunningham Dance Foundation.*
A video piece by Merce Cunningham featuring members of his company, originally taped in the Cunningham studio in New York. The visual quality of this film (of necessity transferred three generations down from the original half-inch videotape) is poor, but the dancing, choreography, and point of view are clear.

The work is carefully and cleanly structured with the choreography specifically arranged for the camera perspective. It begins and ends with views of the studio and has six major sections: 1) the dancers are visually introduced in lingering closeups (in which they seem rather camera conscious); 2) the sculp-tural effect of their massed bodies is explored; 3) they dance a beautiful eight-minute sequence of shifting solos, duets, trios, and quartets; 4) they are seen in conversational profile, four at a time, while two others, in the distance, hop out a chipper pattern; 5) five of them stroll into the studio for a sequence of simultaneous solos, each contrasting spurts of movement with calm poses; and 6) shots of group clusterings are alternated with shots of the entire group zigzagging its way closer and closer to the camera until, at the end, the camera itself joins in the frolic. Cunningham himself does not appear except as a silhouette at the end, a wry signature.

Technically, the film illustrates the perils of trying to work with half-inch videotape. The quality of the picture varies from camera to camera so that there is a noticeable visual jolt whenever there is a cut from one view to another. The sound is rather odd, even by Cunningham standards. Some portions have no sound at all (perhaps the voiced instructions of the choreographer were erased), while others have the live sounds of the dancers in the studio mixed with occasional piano chords.

The dancers, in order of appearance, are Meg Harper, Chris Komar, Cathy Kerr, Robert Kovitch, Ellen Cornfield, Charles Moulton, Valda Setterfield, Julie Roess-Smith, Brynar Mehl, Karen Attix, and George Titus.

## WINNING. 30 min., 1975, color, videotape.*

*Available from ZMC Productions, 245 E. 40 Street, NYC 10016; (212) 661-1587.*
A documentary on the Varna ballet competition of 1974 in which Fernando Bujones won a gold medal. Many dancing clips.

## WITH MY RED FIRES. 31 min., 1978, color.**

*Rental $22, sale $360 from Rochester.*
Doris Humphrey's staggering dance-drama of possessive and vindictive maternal love in a harshly ritualistic and demagogic society, choreographed in 1936. Music by Wallingford Riegger.

Reconstructed from Labanotation by Christine Clark and beautifully performed in 1972 by the professional Repertory Company of the American Dance Festival, Connecticut College, led by Dalienne Majors as the Matriarch, Nina Watt and Raymond Johnson as the Lovers, and Marc Stevens as the Herald.

This film is edited from three camera perspectives. A record version of the film is also available (see below). For Humphrey's thinking on the work, see Selma Jeanne Cohen, *Doris Humphrey: An Artist First*, pp. 140-141.

WITH MY RED FIRES—RECORD FILM. 31 min., 1978, color.*

*Rental $22, sale $360 from Rochester.*

A record version of the same performance as above. The single fixed camera keeps the entire stage in view at all times and permits an appreciation of Humphrey's incredible command of group patterns and of the stage space, though it loses some of the detail and force of the individual movements. To appreciate fully this Humphrey masterpiece, both films should be viewed. (The two films can be rented together from Rochester for a reduced rate of $32.) For suggestions about showing record films like this, see p. 9.)

WORLD'S YOUNG BALLET. 70 min., 1969, b/w.*

*Rental $65 (higher for large audiences or where admission is charged) from Audio Brandon. Five-year lease for $750 from Audio Brandon.*

A Soviet-made documentary on the First International Competition of Ballet Artists held in Moscow in June, 1969. The film shows many of the contestants, including most of the medal winners in action, performing for the judges on the Bolshoi Theatre's bare stage, usually to piano music.

The camera work on the danced portions is generally adequate though most of the sequences are shown only in excerpts and some are belabored by mindless closeups of fancy footwork. Interspersed with these performances are various scenes of the participants warming up, napping, rehearsing, touring, being massaged, gossiping, eating ice cream cones, worrying, and lining up to receive their medals.

Contestants were expected to present several classical numbers in the course of the competition. This meant an inevitable parade of classroom variations (there must have been a million fouettés, but the film, mercifully perhaps, shows only a few). The dancers were also expected to display one "modern" work. Most of these were of such stupefying banality that the judges decided to award no prize for choreography.

The twenty judges, headed by the dignified Galina Ulanova, came from all over the world. One of them, Agnes de Mille, has written a characteristically lively and pungent account of the ordeal in *Dance Perspectives* No. 44 (other valuable accounts by John Barker and Beth Dean were published in the August 1969 issue of *DM*). Among the other judges were Arnold Haskell, Yvette Chauviré, Flemming Flindt, Aram Khachaturian, Alicia Alonso, Yuri Grigorovich, and Maya Plisetskaya.

Participants in the competition did not generally represent their countries in an official sense, but more or less came on their own. The Soviet Ministry of Culture paid transportation one way—round trip if they were among the winners. The bulk of them came from the USSR and East Europe. Western ballet was singularly underrepresented due, in part, to the distaste for such competitions in many circles. For example, there were no dancers at all from Britain, Canada, Australia, or Sweden and only a few from the United States.

The dance material shown is as follows:

1. Parts of the *Black Swan* adagio danced sequentially by three different couples: Loipa Araujo (a silver medal winner) and Azari Plisetski from Cuba, a pair of Hungarians, and gold medal winners Francesca Zumbo and Patrice Bart of France.

2. Alexander Bogatirev (bronze medal) of the Bolshoi in a neatly delivered solo from *Paquita*.

3. The young Kunikova of Perm in an impish solo.

4. Mikhail Baryshnikov (gold medal winner), then of the Kirov, in a solo from *La Bayadère*. Though he is an even better dancer now, the extraordinarily controlled brilliance and the seemingly preparationless springs into the air were already there to be seen in this twenty-year-old dancer.

5. Hideo Fukagawa (silver medal) of Japan in a soaring solo from *Paquita*.

6. Peter Schaufuss (now of the Canadian Ballet) and Anna Marie Duddal-Nielson of Denmark in parts of Bournonville's *Flower Festival* pas de deux.

7. Malika Sabirova (gold medal) in solos from *Don Quixote* and *Corsaire*. Interspersed are some scenes of the dancer being coached by her teacher, Ulanova—a rather startling disclosure since the steely, brittle Sabirova is about as unlike Ulanova as a dancer could be.

8. Yukiko Yasuda and Ishii Jun of Japan, winners of bronze medals, in the *Don Quixote* coda.

9. Alicia Alonso rehearsing Marta Garcia and Jorge Esquival of Cuba in the *Don Quixote* adagio.

10. Moscow's Ludmilla Semenyaka and Nikolai Kovmir, winners of bronze medals, in portions of *Giselle*, Act II, and in a jazzy, goofy, innocent "modern" duet called *Us*.

11. Two Hungarians, Maria Aradi and partner, in an ankle-caressing duet from *Spartacus* (Hungarian choreography).

12. Sections of a duet by Weber, as staged by Maurice Béjart and danced by Esquival and Araujo of Cuba.

13. Portions of a duet to Claude Debussy's *La Mer*, choreographed by Tom Shilling and danced by two East Germans.

14. Baryshnikov in portions of the tour-de-force solo, *Vestris*, that he later revived in the West. He is also seen rehearsing the work with the Soviet choreographer, Leonide Jacobson.

15. Bronze medal winners Natalia Bolshakova and Vadim Gulyaev of the Kirov in excerpts from a

romantic duet to Jules Massenet by veteran Soviet choreographer Kasyan Goleizovsky.

16. Helgi Tomasson (silver medal), then of the Harkness Ballet, in a sparkling, Balanchinesque variation apparently choreographed by Anton Dolin.

17. Zumbo and Bart of Paris in extensive portions of Béjart's flashy and rather erotic *Bhakti*. The duet caused quite a fuss at the competition and some judges wanted to give it an award for choreography, but they were out-voted by those who found it scandalous and/or ill-fitting to the spiritual Indian music it uses.

18. Finally, gold medal winners Nina Sorokina and Yuri Vladimirov of the Bolshoi are shown emoting their way through chunks of *Peace and War* and hurtling themselves through the variations and coda of the *Esmeralda* (or *Diana and Acteon*) *Pas de Deux*.

## YOUNG MAN AND DEATH (JEUNE HOMME ET LA MORT). 15 min., 1965, color.**

*Rental $7 from Kent State, $8.50 from Illinois, $12 from FACSEA. Rental $20, sale $220 from Audio Brandon.*

A somewhat revised version of the 1946 Roland Petit ballet, directed for French television by the choreographer. It is brilliantly danced by Rudolf Nureyev and Petit's wife, "Zizi" Jeanmaire, in the roles originally created by, and strongly identified with, Jean Babilée and Nathalie Philippart.

Rudolf Nureyev and Zizi Jeanmaire in YOUNG MAN AND DEATH

The ballet, based on a scenario by Jean Cocteau, more or less concerns a young man who waits impatiently for a girl in his Paris garret, only to find her cold and rejecting. At her contemptuous suggestion, he hangs himself and, in a kind of apotheosis that is

not included in the film (an improvement, probably), he is led across the rooftops by the figure of death— the girl. The music, chosen to be contrasting and coterminous, rather than accompanying, is Bach's magisterial *Passacaglia and Fugue in C Minor*.

Since the concept and the sensation-ridden choreography, sultry and perverse, are rather dated, the work requires great performances to be effective, and it certainly gets them on this film. Nureyev's shirtless young man is suitably intense and bewildered (Nureyev does bewildered better than almost anybody), and Petit has altered the choreography to allow for plenty of the dancer's spectacular space-devouring vaults. Jeanmaire is at once effectively menacing and seductive.

Except for a few cuts between cameras that are a bit spatially confusing, Petit's camera direction is superb. For an illustrated article on the film, see the April 1968 issue of *DM*. A book, *Nureyev in Paris*, portrays in text and pictures the making of this film. It is available for $10 in bookstores or from the publisher, Modernismo, 233 W. 26 Street, NYC 10001.

## Some films on mime

THE ART OF SILENCE. Thirteen films, 1975, color.

*Each can be rented for from $6 to $9 (depending on length) from Michigan, Indiana, or Minnesota.*

Featuring Marcel Marceau, the films are: BIP AS A SOLDIER (17 min.), BIP AS A SKATER (8 min.), BIP AT A SOCIETY PARTY (14 min.), BIP HUNTS BUTTERFLIES (10 min.), THE CAGE (9 min.), THE CREATION OF THE WORLD (11 min.), THE DREAM (9 min.), THE HANDS (7 min.), THE MASKMAKER (9 min.), THE PAINTER (8 min.), PANTOMIME: LANGUAGE OF THE HEART (10 min.), THE SIDESHOW (9 min.), YOUTH, MATURITY, OLD AGE, DEATH (8 min.).

DINNER PARTY. 7 min., 1958, b/w.

*Rental $8.50 from South Florida.*
Marcel Marceau.

FABLE. 17 min., 1973, color.

*Rental $6 from South Florida, $9.50 from Minnesota, $9.75 from Michigan, $14 from Syracuse.*
Marcel Marceau.

I AM A MIME. 10 min., 1971, color.

*Rental $6.20 from Minnesota, $6.40 from Illinois, $8 from Syracuse.*
An introduction by Antonin Hodek.

IMAGINATION AT WORK. 21 min., 1959, b/w.

*Rental $6 from South Florida.*
About a mime who inherits a brick factory.

IN THE PARK (UN JARDIN PUBLIC). 14 min., b/w.

*Rental $6.80 from Minnesota, $8.50 from South Florida, $12 from FACSEA.*
Marcel Marceau interprets the different characters to be found in a public garden.

MARCEAU ON MIME. 23 min., 1971, color.

*Rental $8.50 from Kent State, $11 from Illinois.*

MARCEL MARCEAU OU L'ART DU MIME. 17 min., b/w.

*Rental $12 from FACSEA.*
Marceau at home, surrounded by documents that trace the history of pantomime. He is also shown on stage performing in Bip and Don Juan.

MARCEL MARCEAU'S PANTOMIMES. 10 min., 1956, color.

*Rental $5.50 from Kent State.*
Performances of David and Goliath, the Butterfly Chase, and the Lion Tamer.

MIME. 29 min., 1966, b/w.

*Rental $6.60 from Minnesota, $11 from Penn State.*
Tony Montanaro discusses mime and is seen in performance.

MIME OF MARCEL MARCEAU. 22 min., 1972, color.

*Rental $8.50 from Kent State, $10.90 from Minnesota, $11.40 from Illinois, $12.50 from Penn State, $15 from UCLA, $15 from Budget, $16 from Syracuse. Sale $310 from LCA.*
Marceau in performance and rehearsal.

MIME OVER MATTER. 12 min., 1972, color.

*Rental $6.60 from Iowa, $10 from Syracuse.*
Czech mime Ladislav Fialka.

PANTOMIMES. 20 min., 1954, color, silent.

*Rental $12 from FACSEA.*
Marcel Marceau in a number of acts: playing dice; adolescence, maturity, old age; Bip as David and Goliath; chasing butterflies; the tamer. Preface by Jean Cocteau.

# Some recommended ethnic dance films

Listed below are ten good films showing a wide variety of non-western and ethnic dance. There are scores, perhaps hundreds, of ethnic dance films available. Two rental libraries with considerable holdings in this area are California and Penn State. (The latter has the extensive *Encyclopedia Cinematographia* series for rental.) Anyone with a special interest should consult their catalogs as well as the *Catalog of Dance Films* published by Dance Films Association, 250 W. 57 Street, NYC 10019. See also the items available for purchase on videotape under the CAMERA THREE listing above.

BAYANIHAN. 58 min., color.

*Rental $30.10 from Southern Illinois.*
Philippine dances.

BHARATA NATYAM. 10 min., 1953, b/w.

*Rental $10 from California.*
Indian classic dance.

DANCE AND HUMAN HISTORY. 40 min., 1976, color.

*Rental $28, sale $415 from California.*
A compilation by Alan Lomax.

DANCE CONTEST IN ESIRA. 11 min., 1936, b/w.

*Rental $15 from MOMA.*
Madagascar tribes.

FIVE ABORIGINAL DANCES FROM CAPE YORK. 9 min., 1966, color.

*Rental $2.50 from Australian Information Service, 635 Fifth Avenue, NYC 10020, (212) 245-4000; $5.50 from Indiana.*

KABUKI: CLASSIC THEATRE OF JAPAN. 30 min., color.

*Rental free from Association (ask for film No. 19011).*

A NIGHT AT THE PEKING OPERA. 20 min., 1960, color.

*Rental $6.80 from Minnesota, $9 from Michigan, $9.35 from Iowa, $9.85 from Northern Illinois, $11.50 from Illinois, $12.50 from Penn State. Sale $275 from Radim.*

SPANISH GYPSIES. 11 min., 1947, b/w.

> *Rental $10 from Radim.*
> Juan Salido and others.

SUITE OF BERBER DANCES. 10 min., b/w.

> *Rental $5 from Indiana, $10 from Radim.*
> Morocco.

TRANCE AND DANCE IN BALI. 20 min., b/w.

> *Rental $4.60 from Minnesota, $5.30 from Michigan, $6.35 from Northern Illinois, $6.60 from Iowa, $6.70 from Illinois, $13 from California.*
> Narrated by Margaret Mead.

# The film musicals of Fred Astaire

Below is a list of the film musicals of Fred Astaire (b. 1899) in the order in which the films were made. They are generally available, at rentals of between $33 and $100, from these sources: Films Incorporated (FI), Universal/16 (U/16), Audio Brandon (AB), Budget Films (BF), Association (Ass'n), ROA, or Swank. Rentals from Films Inc. and Universal/16 should be taken as a minimum guarantee as against fifty percent of any admission receipts; rentals from Budget, Audio Brandon, ROA, Swank, and Association are simply a flat rate. Films from Universal/16 and from Films Inc. can also be rented at a lower rate for classroom showings.

Probably the best single film to start with in the series is TOP HAT, an Astaire/Rogers classic that is available at a relatively low rental. Of course, any Astaire film has at least one number of considerable dance interest (except for FINIAN'S RAINBOW which is included in the list only for the sake of completeness). The economically-priced SECOND CHORUS, YOU'LL NEVER GET RICH, and YOU WERE NEVER LOVELIER all have fine dance numbers and engaging comedy plots.

For analysis and commentary, see Arlene Croce, *The Fred Astaire & Ginger Rogers Book*, and Morton Eustis, "Fred Astaire," *Theater Arts Monthly*, May 1937. Stanley Green and Burt Goldblatt, *Starring Fred Astaire*, is helpful and Astaire's autobiography, *Steps in Time*, is also well worth looking at.

| Release year | Dancing Partner | Rental source | Title, Running Time |
|---|---|---|---|
| 1933 | Crawford | FI $60 | Dancing Lady (90 min.) |
| 1933 | Rogers | FI $75 | Flying Down to Rio (89 min.) |
| 1934 | Rogers | FI $75 | Gay Divorcee (107 min.) |
| 1935 | Rogers | FI $75 | Roberta (105 min.) |
| 1935 | Rogers | AB $45, Ass'n $45 | Top Hat (101 min.) |
| 1936 | Rogers | FI $75 | Follow the Fleet (110 min.) |
| 1936 | Rogers | FI $75 | Swing Time (103 min.) |
| 1937 | Rogers | FI $75 | Shall We Dance (116 min.) |
| 1937 | Burns & Allen | FI $55 | A Damsel in Distress (100 min.) |
| 1938 | Rogers | FI $75 | Carefree (83 min.) |
| 1939 | Rogers | FI $75 | Story of Vernon and Irene Castle (90 min.) |
| 1940 | E. Powell | FI $75 | Broadway Melody of 1940 (102 min.) |
| 1940 | Goddard | See below | Second Chorus (84 min.) |
| 1941 | Hayworth | BF $32.50, Swank $75 | You'll Never Get Rich (88 min.) |
| 1942 | Reynolds | U/16 ? | Holiday Inn (100 min.) |
| 1942 | Hayworth | BF $32.50, Swank $75 | You Were Never Lovelier (98 min.) |
| 1943 | Leslie | FI $50 | The Sky's the Limit (89 min.) |
| 1945 | Bremer | FI $85 | Yolanda and the Thief (108 min., color) |
| 1946 | Bremer, Kelly | FI $100 | Ziegfeld Follies (110 min., color) |
| 1946 | Crosby | U/16 $50 | Blue Skies (104 min., color) |
| 1948 | Garland | FI $75 | Easter Parade (103 min., color) |
| 1949 | Rogers | FI $75 | Barkleys of Broadway (109 min., color) |
| 1950 | Vera-Ellen | FI $75 | Three Little Words (103 min., color) |
| 1950 | Hutton | ? | Let's Dance (111 min., color) |
| 1951 | J. Powell | FI $75 | Royal Wedding (93 min., color) |
| 1952 | Vera-Ellen | FI $50 | Belle of New York (82 min., color) |
| 1953 | Charisse | FI $100 | The Band Wagon (111 min., color) |
| 1955 | Caron | FI $85 | Daddy Long Legs (126 min., color, cinemascope) |
| 1957 | A. Hepburn | FI $75 | Funny Face (103 min., color, Vista Vision) |
| 1957 | Charisse | FI $75 | Silk Stockings (117 min., color, cinemascope) |
| 1968 | None | BF $48, AB $50, Ass'n $50, ROA $55 | Finian's Rainbow (145 min., color, Panavision) |
| 1974 | Multiple | FI $250 | That's Entertainment (131 min., color) |
| 1976 | Multiple | FI Apply | That's Entertainment, Part 2 (133 min., color) |

SECOND CHORUS is the only Astaire film to have fallen into public domain and is, accordingly, widely and cheaply available. It can be rented for $20 from Budget, for $25 from Em Gee, $25 from ROA. It can be purchased on 16mm for around $200 from Steiglitz Film Market, P.O. Box 127, Bay Ridge Station, Brooklyn, NY 11220; from Hollywood Film Exchange, 1534 No. Highland Avenue, Hollywood, CA 90028; from Cinema Concepts, 91 Main Street, Chester, CT 06412; from Thunderbird; or from Nostalgia Films, P.O. Box 666 Gracie Station, NYC 10028. The film is also available on 8mm from these distributors.

Some six minutes of dance clips from SECOND CHORUS can be rented under the title, GREAT ASTAIRE, for $5 from Kit Parker, $7.50 from Association, or for $9 from South Florida. They can be purchased for $33 from Cinema Concepts (address above) or for $40 from Association. Extracts from two other Astaire films can be rented for $7 each from Kent State (or together for $40 from Films, Inc.): GAY DIVORCEE (a 19 min. section that includes the complete "Continental" number) and FUNNY FACE (14 min. of excerpts including the "Funny Face" song and dance, the "He Loves and She Loves" number, the scene where an Astaire-Hepburn argument ruins an elaborate fashion show, and the conclusion with a reprise of "He Loves and She Loves").

As a short to follow a showing of TOP HAT, Buster Keaton's GRAND SLAM OPERA (20 min., 1936, b/w) is strongly recommended. Probably the best of Keaton's sound shorts, the film includes a galumphing parody of the "No Strings" number in TOP HAT. The Keaton short rents for $6.50 from Em Gee.

# Busby Berkeley films

Below is a list of the 1930s films featuring large production numbers by Busby Berkeley. They are available from UA/16: the three from 1933 rent for $125 ($75 classroom), the others for $75 ($60 classroom).

The Berkeley film usually considered to be his classic is the one that started it all, 42ND STREET. The number considered by Berkeley (and just about everyone else) to be his best is the hard-edged, surrealistic "Lullaby of Broadway" from GOLD DIGGERS OF 1935. The best of the "plotless" numbers is probably "Don't Say Goodnight" from WONDER BAR (a film that also includes the appalling blackface "Goin' to Heaven on a Mule"). For commentary, see John Herbert McDowell, "Movie Musicals," *Ballet Review*, Vol. 2, No 2, and Tony Thomas and Jim Terry, *The Busby Berkeley Book* (1973).

42ND STREET. 1933, 90 min., b/w.

Baxter, Powell, Keeler, Rogers. Numbers: *Shuffle Off to Buffalo, Young and Healthy* (legs), *42nd Street.*

GOLD DIGGERS OF 1933. 1933, 94 min., b/w.

Powell, Keeler, Rogers, Blondell. Numbers: *We're in the Money, Pettin' in the Park, Shadow Waltz* (electric violins), *Forgotten Man.*

FOOTLIGHT PARADE. 1933, 104 min., b/w.

Cagney, Blondell, Keeler, Powell. Numbers: *Honeymoon Hotel, By a Waterfall, Shanghai Lil.*

WONDER BAR. 1934, 90 min.

Jolson, Powell, Francis, Del Rio. Numbers: *Don't Say Goodnight* (mirrors, pillars), *Goin' to Heaven on a Mule.*

FASHIONS OF 1934. 1934, 80 min., b/w.

Powell, Davis. Numbers: *Spin a Little Web of Dreams* (ostrich feathers), *Broken Melody.*

DAMES. 1934, 90 min.

Blondell, Powell, Keeler. Numbers: *Girl at the Ironing Board, I Only Have Eyes for You* (Keeler posters), *Dames.*

GOLD DIGGERS OF 1935. 1935, 95 min., b/w.

Powell, Menjou, Stuart, Shaw. Numbers: *The Words Are in My Heart* (pianos), *Lullaby of Broadway* (nightclub with hundreds of dancers, audience of two).

GOLD DIGGERS OF 1937. 1937, 100 min., b/w.

Powell, Blondell. Number: *All's Fair in Love and War* (rocking chairs).

Related shorts:

HOLLYWOOD NEWSREEL. 1934, 10 min., b/w.

*Rental $20 from UA/16.*
A look around the set during filming of WONDER BAR.

CALLING ALL GIRLS. 1935, 18 min., b/w.

*Rental $10 from Budget, $15 from Audio Brandon, $25 from UA/16.*
Behind scenes in filming Berkeley productions,

including auditions. Includes clips of *By a Waterfall*, *Lullaby of Broadway*, *Shadow Waltz*, *Shanghai Lil*.

## A TRIP THROUGH A HOLLYWOOD STUDIO. 1936, 10 min., b/w.

*Rental $20 from UA/16.*
Includes scenes of Berkeley at work.

## THREE CHEERS FOR THE GIRLS. 1943, 18 min., b/w.

*Rental $10 from Budget, $15 from Audio Brandon.*
A Berkeley-created short.

## FABULOUS HOLLYWOOD MUSICALS. 1963, 23 min., b/w.

*Rental $17.50 from Em Gee.*
A Wolper documentary on 1930s musicals including Berkeley, Astaire.

# Hollywood musicals with choreography by George Balanchine

## GOLDWYN FOLLIES (United Artists). 115 min., 1938, b/w.

*Rental $45 from Budget, $45 from ROA, $50 from Twyman, $50 (higher for large audiences or where admission is charged) from Audio Brandon or from Association.*
There are two fine dance numbers in this feature, each seven minutes long. *Romeo and Juliet*, done on a stage, features a battle between a ballet corps and a corps of jazz dancers and includes an unconventional adagio for Vera Zorina and partner notable for its quick, fluid lifts. *Water Nymph Ballet* is set in a fanciful outdoor dance area with a pool in its center around which a group dances. Zorina rises from the pool, does a narcissistic solo, and is pursued by one of the men. They are separated by a choreographed confusion and a heavy wind storm and she descends back into the pool as he watches from afar. Except for its interpolated Gershwin songs ("Love Walked In" and "Love Is Here to Stay"), the film's plot is a predictable, pulverizing bore.

## ON YOUR TOES (Warner Bros.). 94 min., 1939, b/w.

*Rental $35 from UA/16.*
A film version of the Rodgers and Hart Broadway musical (for which Balanchine also did the stage choreography) with much of the music left out. One dance number is a parody of *Scheherazade* featuring an exotic adagio, and the other is the famous *Slaughter on Tenth Avenue*. Vera Zorina dances the role created on stage by Tamara Geva. Regrettably, Hollywood brought in a non-dancer, Eddie Albert, for the role of the tapper originated on the stage by Ray Bolger.

## I WAS AN ADVENTURESS (20th Century-Fox). 90 min., 1940, b/w.

*Rental $35 from Films Inc.*
The lone dance number is a seven-minute fantasy-parody of *Swan Lake*. The Prince (dressed in armor) is Lew Christensen, the Swan Queen who finally vanishes from his arms is Vera Zorina. The choreography is very camera-aware; there is a brief passage in which the corps cascades toward the camera which is especially impressive. At the end, the abandoned Prince clanks his way out into the lake and sobs on the distant castle which proves to be a miniature. Balanchine, though uncredited as an actor, appears twice in the film as the conductor of a pit orchestra—he even has a line or two. The plot, written in part by John O'Hara, is excellent. It concerns some international jewel thieves (Zorina, Erich Von Stroheim, and Peter Lorre) and is filled with unexpected twists and turns.

## STAR-SPANGLED RHYTHM (Paramount). 99 min., 1942, b/w.

*Rental $40 from Universal/16 (classroom lower).*
The film is a many-starred revue. Balanchine's contribution was an exotic number, *That Old Black Magic*, for Vera Zorina.

# Indexes

## Film distributors

Note: All rental fees are for *one* day's use unless otherwise indicated.

ACI

    ACI Films, Inc.
    35 West 45th St.
    New York, NY 10036
    (212) 582-1918

Association

    Association Films
    866 Third Ave.
    New York, NY 10022
      (10 offices nationwide)
    (212) 935-4210

    In Canada:
    333 Adelaide St.
    Toronto, Ontario
    (416) EM2-2501

Audio Brandon (five addresses)

    Macmillan Audio Brandon
    34 MacQuesten Parkway So.
    Mount Vernon, NY 10550
    (914) 664-5051

    3868 Piedmond Ave.
    Oakland, CA 94611
    (415) 658-9890

    1619 North Cherokee
    Los Angeles, CA 90028
    (213) 463-0357

    2512 Program Drive
    Dallas, TX 75229
    (214) 357-6494

    8400 Brookfield Ave.
    Brookfield, IL 60513
    (312) 485-3925

BFA

    BFA Educational Media
    2211 Michigan Ave.
    Santa Monica, CA 90406

Boston (low postage charges)

    Boston University Film Library
    765 Commonwealth Ave.
    Boston, MA 02215
    (617) 353-3272

Bouchard

    Thomas Bouchard
    Stony Brook Road
    West Brewster, Cape Cod, MA 02631
    (617) 896-3708

Budget (rentals 10% higher outside the 11 western states)

    Budget Films
    4590 Santa Monica Blvd.
    Los Angeles, CA 90029
    (213) 660-0187

California

    Extension Media Center
    University of California
    Berkeley, CA 94720
    (415) 642-0460

Celebrity

    William Justin, Campus Division
    Celebrity Concert Corporation
    315 South Beverly Drive
    Beverly Hills, CA 90212
    (213) 553-0111

Cunningham Dance Foundation

    Cunningham Dance Foundation
    463 West Street
    New York, NY 10014
    (212) 255-8240

Dance Films (rental only to members, membership is $15 per year; sale to all)

    Dance Films Association, Inc.
    250 West 57th St.
    New York, NY 10019
    (212) 586-2142

East End

    East End Film Co.
    Box 275
    Wainscott, NY 11975
    (516) 537-0178

Em Gee

    Em Gee Film Library
    16024 Ventura Blvd.
    Encino, CA 91436
    (213) 981-5506

FACSEA

Society for French American Cultural Services &
Educational Aid
972 Fifth Ave.
New York, NY 10021
(212) RE7-9700

Films Inc. (many features available at lower classroom rates)

Films Incorporated
733 Greenbay Rd.
Wilmette, IL 60091
(312) 256-6600

440 Park Ave. So.
New York, NY 10016
(212) 889-7910

5589 New Peachtree Rd.
Atlanta, GA 30341
(404) 451-7431

5625 Hollywood Blvd.
Hollywood, CA 90028
(213) 466-5481

FMC

Film-Maker's Cooperative
175 Lexington Ave.
New York, NY 10016
(212) 889-3820

Grove

Grove Press Film Division
53 East 11th St.
New York, NY 10003
(212) 677-2400

Heritage

Heritage Visual Sales
508 Church St.
Toronto, Ontario M4Y 2C8
(416) 966-5222

Illinois (rental price is for 1 week's use; postal charges
low)

Visual Aids Service
University of Illinois
Champaign, IL 61820
(217) 333-1360

Indiana (rental price is for 1 week's use; postal charges
low)

Audio-Visual Center
Indiana University
Bloomington, IN 47401
(812) 337-2103

Iowa (rental price is for 3 days' use)

Audio-Visual Center
University of Iowa
Iowa City, IA 52242
(319) 353-5885

Kent State (rental price is for 3 days' use)

Audio-Visual Services
Kent State University
Kent, OH 44242
(216) 672-3456

Kentucky

Audio-Visual Services
University of Kentucky
Lexington, KY 40406

Kit Parker

Kit Parker Films
Carmel Valley, CA 93924
(408) 659-4131

LCA

Learning Corporation of America
1350 Ave. of the Americas
New York, NY 10019
(212) 751-4400

McGraw-Hill

McGraw-Hill/Contemporary Films
1221 Ave. of the Americas
New York, NY 10020

Michigan (rental price is for up to 3 days' use)

University of Michigan
Audio-Visual Education Center
416 Fourth St.
Ann Arbor, MI 48103
(313) 764-5361

Minnesota (rental price is for up to 5 days' use;
postal charges low, out-of-state orders: $5 surcharge)

Audio-Visual Library Service
3300 University Ave., S.E.
University of Minnesota
Minneapolis, MN 55414
(612) 373-3810

Modern Talking Picture Service

Modern Talking Picture Service
315 Springfield Ave.
Summit, NJ 07901
(201) 277-6300

2323 New Hyde Park Rd.
New Hyde Park, NY 11040
(516) 437-6300

1687 Elmhurst Rd.
Chicago, IL 60007

MOMA

Museum of Modern Art Department of Film
11 West 53rd St.
New York, NY 10019
(212) 956-6100

NCA-SF

National Council of American-Soviet Friendship
156 Fifth Ave.
Suite 304
New York, NY 10010
(212) YU9-6677

Northern Illinois (rental price is for up to 5 days' use)

Media Distribution
Northern Illinois University
DeKalb, IL 60115
(815) 753-0171

Ohio State

Film Distribution Supervisor
Ohio State University
Department of Photography and Cinema
156 West 19th Ave.
Columbus, OH 43210

Pennebaker

Pennebaker, Inc.
56 West 45th St.
New York, NY 10036
(212) 986-7020

Penn State

Pennsylvania State University
Audio-Visual Services
University Park, PA 16802

Phoenix

Phoenix Films, Inc.
470 Park Ave. So.
New York, NY 10016
(212) 684-5910

International Tele-Film Enterprises
47 Densley Ave.
Toronto, Ontario M6M 5A8
(416) 241-4483

Pyramid

Pyramid Films
Box 1048
Santa Monica, CA 90406
(213) 828-7577

Radim

Radim Films, Inc./Film Images
1034 Lake St.
Oak Park, IL 60301
(312) 386-4826

17 West 60th St.
New York, NY 10023
(212) 279-6653

ROA

ROA Films
1696 N. Astor St.
Milwaukee, WI 53202
(414) 271-0861

Rochester

Dance Film Archive
University of Rochester
Rochester, NY 14627

Schoenfeld

Schoenfeld Film Distributing Corp.
165 West 46th St.
New York, NY 10036
(212) 765-8977

Select

Select Film Library
115 West 31st St.
New York, NY 10001
(212) 594-4457

South Florida (rental price is for up to 3 days' use)

Films
Educational Resources
University of South Florida
Tampa, FL 33620
(813) 974-2341

Southern Illinois

Learning Resources Service
Southern Illinois University
Carbondale, IL 62901
(618) 453-2258

Steeg

Ted Steeg
41 West 56th St.
New York, NY 10019
(212) LT1-8471

Swank (rather expensive postage charges)

Swank Films
393 Front St.
Hempstead, NY 11550
(516) 538-6500

Syracuse (rental price is for a 2-day period; rentals higher outside the northeast and southeast)

Film Rental Center
Syracuse University
Syracuse, NY 13210
(315) 479-6631
(315) 423-2452

Thunderbird

Thunderbird Films
P.O. Box 65157
Los Angeles, CA 90065

Time-Life

Time-Life Films
100 Eisenhower Dr.
Paramus, NJ 07652
(201) 843-4545

Tricontinental

Tricontinental Film Center
333 Ave. of the Americas
New York, NY 10014
(212) 989-3330

P.O. Box 4430
Berkeley, CA 94704
(415) 548-3204

Twyman

Twyman Films
Box 605
Dayton, OH 45401
(800) 543-9594 (toll free)
in Ohio (513) 222-4014 (call collect)

UA/16

UA/16
729 Seventh Ave.
New York, NY 10019
(212) 575-4715

UCLA (charges expensive postal rates)

UCLA Media Center
Instructional Media Library
Los Angeles, CA 90024
(213) 825-0755

Universal/16

Universal/16
445 Park Ave.
New York, NY 10022
(212) 759-7500 x244, 301, 505

5 US offices: Atlanta, Chicago, Dallas, Los Angeles, N.Y.
3 Canadian offices: Toronto, Montreal, St. John NB

USC (rental price is for up to 3 days' use)

University of Southern California
Division of Cinema, Film Distribution Section
University Park
Los Angeles, CA 90007
(213) 746-2235

Utah (rental price is for 3 days' use)

Education Media Center
U. of Utah
Salt Lake City, UT 84110
(801) 581-6112

Viewfinders

Viewfinders
Box 1665
Evanston, IL 60204
(312) 869-0602

Weber

Anthony Weber Enterprises
11608-1/2 Washington Blvd.
Los Angeles, CA 90066
(213) 391-4375

## Index of choreographers

Listed below are choreographers whose works are available on film, together with the title, or shortened title, of the film or films on which they are represented, and the page number(s) in the Directory. Cine-dance filmmakers are also included in this index. (See also the choreographers in the list, VIDEO EXCHANGE.)

Ailey, Alvin: ALVIN AILEY, 20; AMERICAN BALLET THEATRE, 21

Alonso, Alberto: ALICIA, 20

Arpino, Gerald: ATTITUDES IN DANCE, 23; DANCE: ROBERT JOFFREY BALLET, 35

Shawn, Ted: RUTH ST. DENIS AND TED SHAWN, 58; RUTH ST. DENIS BY BARIBAULT, 58

Sokolow, Anna: ANNA SOKOLOW DIRECTS—ODES, 23; DANCE: ANNA SOKOLOW'S ROOMS, 32; DANCE: ROBERT JOFFREY BALLET, 35; OPUS OP, 53

Takei, Kei: LIGHT, PART 5, 47

Tamiris, Helen: HELEN TAMIRIS IN HER NEGRO SPIRITUALS, 42

Taylor, Paul: JUNCTION, 45; PAUL TAYLOR AND CO., 55

Terry, Walter: GREAT PERFORMANCE IN DANCE, 42

Tetley, Glen: ANATOMY LESSON, 22; DANCE: IN SEARCH OF "LOVERS," 34; I AM A DANCER, 43

Tharp, Twyla: BIX PIECES, 29; SUE'S LEG, 62

Tudor, Antony: AMERICAN BALLET THEATRE, 21; MODERN BALLET, 51; VERY EYE OF NIGHT, 65

Van Dantzig, Rudi: MAKING OF A BALLET, 47

Wagner, Richard: CAMERA THREE, 30

Walker, Norman: ATTITUDES IN DANCE, 23

Weidman, Charles: FESTIVAL, 40; FLICKERS, 40; NEW DANCE, 52

Wigman, Mary: MARY WIGMAN, 50

Zakharov, Rostislav: BOLSHOI BALLET, 29; CINDERELLA, 31; STARS OF THE RUSSIAN BALLET, 61

## Index of dance works

Listed below are ballet and modern dance works which are available on film, together with the title of the film or films on which they appear and the page number(s) in the Directory. Cine-dance films are not included. They can be found under the name of the filmmaker in the index of choreographers above, or by title in the alphabetical list of films below.

Abyss (complete): REFLECTIONS ON CHOREOGRAPHY, 56

Acrobats of God (complete): ACROBATS OF GOD, 19

Adorations (complete): MARTHA GRAHAM DANCE COMPANY, 48

Afternoon of a Faun (complete): AFTERNOON OF A FAUN, 19

Afternoon of a Faun (excerpt): BALLET FOR ALL—6, 27

Agathe's Tale (excerpt): PAUL TAYLOR AND COMPANY, 55

Agon (excerpt): BOLSHOI BALLET TOURS, 29; DANCE: NEW YORK CITY BALLET, 34

Air for the G String (complete): AIR FOR THE G STRING, 20

Air for the G String (brief excerpt): DANCE: FOUR PIONEERS, 33

Anatomy Lesson (complete): ANATOMY LESSON, 22

Apollo (excerpt): BALLET WITH EDWARD VILLELLA, 28

Appalachian Spring (complete): APPALACHIAN SPRING, 23; MARTHA GRAHAM DANCE COMPANY, 48

As I Lay Dying (complete): CAMERA THREE, 30

Assemblage (complete): ASSEMBLAGE, 23

Aureole (excerpt): PAUL TAYLOR AND COMPANY, 55

Aurora's Wedding (complete): EVENING WITH THE ROYAL BALLET, 39; SLEEPING BEAUTY, 60

Ballet de la Nuit (excerpt): BALLET FOR ALL—1, 26

Ballet for Four (complete): ATTITUDES IN DANCE, 23

Bayaderka (excerpt): BALLET CONCERT, 25; BAYADERKA, 28; WORLD'S YOUNG BALLET, 68

Beau Danube (excerpt): GREAT PERFORMANCE IN DANCE, 42

Beauty and the Beast (complete): BEAUTY AND THE BEAST, 28

Beauty and the Beast (excerpt): SADLER'S WELLS BALLERINA, 58

Bhakti (excerpt): BALLET OF THE 20TH CENTURY, 28; CAMERA THREE, 30; WORLD'S YOUNG BALLET, 68

Les Biches (excerpt): BALLET FOR ALL—6, 27

Biosfera (excerpt): RHYTHMETRON, 56

Birthday Offering (excerpt): MARGOT FONTEYN, 48

Bix Pieces (complete): BIX PIECES, 29

Black and Gold Sari (complete): FIRST LADY OF AMERICAN DANCE, 40

Black Swan Pas de Deux (complete): ALICIA (Alonso), 20; AMERICAN BALLET THEATRE (Gregory), 21; STARS OF THE RUSSIAN BALLET (Dudinskaya), 61; STARS OF THE RUSSIAN BALLET—SWAN LAKE (Dudinskaya), 62; SWAN LAKE (Plisetskaya), 63; SWAN LAKE (Yevteyeva), 63

Black Swan Pas de Deux (excerpt): PLISETSKAYA DANCES; WORLD'S YOUNG BALLET, 68

Blue Studio; 29

Bluebird Pas de Deux (complete): EVENING WITH THE ROYAL BALLET, 39; NUTCRACKER, 53

## Index of dancers

Since there are thousands of different dancers on the films in this directory, this index is, of necessity, somewhat selective. However, it does list just about every dancer given reasonably prominent display in a film. The names of the dancers are followed by the title of the film or films on which they appear and the page number(s) in the Directory.

Driver, Senta: ANNA SOKOLOW DIRECTS—ODES, 23; PAUL TAYLOR AND CO., 55

Dudinskaya, Natalia: BALLET CONCERT, 25; BAYADERKA, 28; CONCERT OF STARS, 31; SLEEPING BEAUTY, 60; STARS OF THE RUSSIAN BALLET, 61 and 62

Duncan, Isadora: see DANCE ON FILM: 1894-1912, Part II, 35; and EARLY DANCE FILMS, 37

Duncan, Jeff: DANCE: ANNA SOKOLOW'S ROOMS, 32

Dunham, Katherine: CARNIVAL OF RHYTHM, 30

Dunn, Douglas: WALKAROUND TIME, 66

Dunn, Judith: INDEX, 45; OFFICIAL DOCTRINE, 53; THREE DANCES, 64

Eglevsky, Andre: CLASSICAL BALLET, 31; GAY PARISIAN, 41; SPANISH FIESTA, 61

Eglevsky, Marina: CLASSICAL BALLET, 31

Eilber, Janet: DAY ON EARTH, 36; MARTHA GRAHAM DANCE COMPANY, 48

Emblem, Ronald: BALLET FOR ALL—7, 27

Erdman, Jean: CAMERA THREE, 30; OUT OF CHAOS, 54

Ericsson, Catharina: SWEDEN, 63

Esquival, Jorge: WORLD'S YOUNG BALLET, 68

Everett, Ellen: AMERICAN BALLET THEATRE, 21

Fadeyechev, Nikolai: BOLSHOI BALLET, 29; PLISETSKAYA DANCES, 55

Farrell, Suzanne: BALLET OF THE 20TH CENTURY, 28; DANCE: NEW YORK CITY BALLET, 34; MIDSUMMER NIGHT'S DREAM, 51; STRAVINSKY, 62

Farron, Julia: ROMEO AND JULIET BALLET, 57

Fialka, Ladislav: MIME OVER MATTER, 70

Flier, Jaap: ANATOMY LESSON, 22

Fokina, Vera: DYING SWAN (stills), 37

Fonteyn, Margot: BEHIND THE SCENES, 28; EVENING WITH THE ROYAL BALLET, 39; I AM A DANCER, 43; MARGOT FONTEYN, 48; MARGOT FONTEYN IN LES SYLPHIDES, 48; ROMEO AND JULIET BALLET, 57; ROYAL BALLET, 57

Fracci, Carla: GISELLE, 42; I AM A DANCER, 43

Franklin, Frederic: GAY PARISIAN, 41; GREAT PERFORMANCE IN DANCE, 42; SPANISH FIESTA, 61

Fuente, Luis: DANCE: ROBERT JOFFREY BALLET, 35

Fukagawa, Hideo: WORLD'S YOUNG BALLET, 68

Gable, Christopher: BEHIND THE SCENES, 28

Garcia-Lorca, Isabel: BIX PIECES, 29

Garland, Judy: see 71

Geltzer, Yekaterina: MODERN BALLET, 51

Goddard, Paulette: see 71

Gollner, Nana: NANA, 52; SPRING NIGHT, 61

Govrin, Gloria: MIDSUMMER NIGHT'S DREAM, 51

Graham, Martha: ACROBATS OF GOD, 19; APPALACHIAN SPRING, 23; CORTEGE OF EAGLES, 31; LAMENTATION, 46; NIGHT JOURNEY, 52

Grahame, Shirley: BALLET FOR ALL—5, 27

Grant, Alexander: ENIGMA VARIATIONS, 38; ROYAL BALLET, 57; STEPS OF THE BALLET, 61

Gregory, Cynthia: AMERICAN BALLET THEATRE, 21; IN A REHEARSAL ROOM, 44

Grinwis, Paul: GRADUATION BALL, 42

Gulyaev, Vadim: WORLD'S YOUNG BALLET, 68

Gusev, Pyotr: SCENES FROM THE BALLET OF FOUNTAIN OF BAKHCHISARAI, 59; STARS OF THE RUSSIAN BALLET, 61

Gutelius, Phyllis: ACROBATS OF GOD, 19; SERAPHIC DIALOGUE, 59

Haight, Elizabeth: DAY ON EARTH, 36

Halprin, Ann: ANN, 23; HALPRIN, 42; PROCESSION, 56

Harper, Meg: VIDEO EVENT, 65; WALKAROUND TIME, 66; WESTBETH, 67

Hatch Walker, David: MARTHA GRAHAM DANCE COMPANY, 48

Hawkins, Erick: ERICK HAWKINS, 38

Hayden, Melissa: DANCE: NEW YORK CITY BALLET, 34; NUTCRACKER, 53; TIME TO DANCE, 64

Hayman-Chaffey, Susana: VIDEO EVENT, 65; WALKAROUND TIME, 66

Hayworth, Rita: see 71

Heinrich, Helga: NUTCRACKER, 53

Helpmann, Robert: DON QUIXOTE, 36; RED SHOES, 56; TALES OF HOFFMANN, 63

Hepburn, Audrey: see 71

Hermans, Emery: FILM WITH THREE DANCERS, 40; IMAGE, FLESH AND VOICE, 43; SCAPEMATES, 58

Hinkson, Mary: ACROBATS OF GOD, 19; CORTEGE OF EAGLES, 31; DANCE: ECHOES OF JAZZ, 33; DANCE: IN SEARCH OF "LOVERS," 34; DANCER'S WORLD, 35; NIGHT JOURNEY, 52; SERAPHIC DIALOGUE, 59

Hodek, Antonin: I AM A MIME, 69

Hodes, Stuart: APPALACHIAN SPRING, 23

Louther, William: ACROBATS OF GOD, 19; COR-TEGE OF EAGLES, 31; DANCE: ECHOES OF JAZZ, 33

Love, Ellen: LAMENT, 46

Luckey, Susan: CAROUSEL, 30

Ludlow, Conrad: MIDSUMMER NIGHT'S DREAM, 51

Lyman, Peggy: MARTHA GRAHAM DANCE COM-PANY, 48

McBride, Patricia: ART IS, 23; BALLET WITH ED-WARD VILLELLA, 28; DANCE: NEW YORK CITY BALLET, 34; MIDSUMMER NIGHT'S DREAM, 51; NUTCRACKER, 53

McCallum, Harlan: LANGUAGE OF DANCE, 46

MacDonald, Gene: DANCER'S WORLD, 35

McGehee, Helen: ACROBATS OF GOD, 19; APPA-LACHIAN SPRING, 23; CORTEGE OF EAGLES, 31; DANCER'S WORLD, 35; NIGHT JOURNEY, 52; SERAPHIC DIALOGUE, 59

McIntyre, Dianne: ANNA SOKOLOW DIRECTS—ODES, 23

Magallanes, Nicholas: MIDSUMMER NIGHT'S DREAM, 51

Majors, Dalienne: WITH MY RED FIRES, 67-68

Makarova, Natalia: SLEEPING BEAUTY, 60

Marceau, Marcel: see 69-70

Markova, Alicia: SUGAR PLUM FAIRY VARIA-TION, 63

Markovsky, John: SWAN LAKE, 63

Martinez, Enrique: DANCE—A REFLECTION OF OUR TIMES, 32

Maslow, Sophie: CAMERA THREE, 30

Massine, Leonide: GAY PARISIAN, 41; RED SHOES, 56; SPANISH FIESTA, 61; TALES OF HOFF-MANN, 63

Mathis, Bonnie: AMERICAN BALLET THEATRE, 21

Mead, Robert: BEHIND THE SCENES, 28; ENIG-MA VARIATIONS, 38; OPUS, 53

Mehl, Brynar: VIDEO EVENT, 65; WESTBETH, 67

Mercier, Margaret: PAS DE DEUX, 54

Miller, Buzz: DANCE: ECHOES OF JAZZ, 33

Miller, Patricia: SADLER'S WELLS BALLERINA, 58

Mitchell, Arthur: DANCE: NEW YORK CITY BAL-LET, 34; MIDSUMMER NIGHT'S DREAM, 51

Mladova, Milada: GAY PARISIAN, 41

Moncion, Francisco: MIDSUMMER NIGHT'S DREAM, 51

Montanaro, Tony: MIME, 70

Monte, Elisa: MARTHA GRAHAM DANCE COM-PANY, 48

Moore, Jack: DANCE: ANNA SOKOLOW'S ROOMS, 32

Moore, Molly: JUNCTION, 45; PAUL TAYLOR AND CO., 55

Morosova, Olga: GRADUATION BALL, 42

Morris, Marnee: BALLET WITH EDWARD VILL-ELLA, 28; DORIS CHASE, 37

Mosaval, Johaar: BALLET FOR ALL—6, 27

Moulton, Charles: VIDEO EVENT, 65; WESTBETH, 67

Nagrin, Daniel: DANCE IN THE SUN, 34; NAGRIN, 52; TIME TO DANCE, 64

Nagy, Ivan: AMERICAN BALLET THEATRE, 21; IN A REHEARSAL ROOM, 44

Nazimova, Alla: SALOME, 58

Neels, Sandra: RAINFOREST, 56; WALKAROUND TIME, 66

Newman, Susannah: ANNA SOKOLOW DIRECTS—ODES, 23

Nightingale, John: PAUL TAYLOR AND CO., 55

Nijinsky, Vaslav: AFTERNOON OF A FAUN (stills), 19

Nureyev, Rudolf: BEHIND THE SCENES, 28; DON QUIXOTE, 36; EVENING WITH THE ROYAL BALLET, 39; I AM A DANCER, 43; MARGOT FONTEYN, 48; ROMEO AND JULIET BALLET, 57; YOUNG MAN AND DEATH, 69

Orloff, Nicolas: BALLERINA, 24

Orr, Terry: AMERICAN BALLET THEATRE, 21

Oved, Margalit: GESTURES OF SAND, 41

Page, Annette: EVENING WITH THE ROYAL BAL-LET, 39

Panov, Valery: SLEEPING BEAUTY, 60; SWAN LAKE, 63

Paredes, Marcos: AMERICAN BALLET THEATRE, 21

Park, Merle: EVENING WITH THE ROYAL BAL-LET, 39

Parkinson, Georgina: ENIGMA VARIATIONS, 38; EVENING WITH THE ROYAL BALLET, 39

Parks, John: ALVIN AILEY, 20

Pate, Maldwyn: LIGHT, PART 5, 47

Paul, Mimi: MIDSUMMER NIGHT'S DREAM, 51

Pavlova, Anna: BALLET FOR ALL—5, 27; GREAT PERFORMANCE IN DANCE, 42; IMMORTAL SWAN, 43

Payton, James: ANNA SOKOLOW DIRECTS—ODES, 23

Woodruff, Dianne: ANNA SOKOLOW DIRECTS—ODES, 23

Workman, Jennie: DANCE—A REFLECTION OF OUR TIMES, 32

Wright, Rose-Marie: BIX PIECES, 29; SUE'S LEG, 62

Yarborough, Sara: ALVIN AILEY, 20

Yasuda, Yukiko: WORLD'S YOUNG BALLET, 68

Yershova, Yevgenia: LILEYA, 47

Yevteyeva, Yelena: SWAN LAKE, 63

Yoneyawa, Mamako: BAGGAGE, 23

Young, Gayle: AMERICAN BALLET THEATRE, 21; FALL RIVER LEGEND, 40

Yourth, Linda: CLASSICAL BALLET, 31

Youskevitch, Igor: GAY PARISIAN, 41; GISELLE, 41; INVITATION TO THE DANCE, 45

Yuan, Tina: ALVIN AILEY, 20

Yuriko: APPALACHIAN SPRING, 23; DANCER'S WORLD, 35

Zhdanov, Yuri: PLISETSKAYA DANCES, 55; ROMEO AND JULIET, 57; SCENES FROM THE BALLET OF FOUNTAIN OF BAKHCHISARAI, 59; STARS OF THE RUSSIAN BALLET, 61

Zorina, Vera: see 73

Zumbo, Francesca: WORLD'S YOUNG BALLET, 68

# Alphabetical list of films

*For key to abbreviations see p. 19.*

ACROBATS OF GOD. 22 min., 1969, color**, 19

ADAGIO (L'ADAGE). 14 min., 1963, b/w*, 19

ADOLESCENCE. 22 min., 1966, b/w*, 19

AFTERNOON OF A FAUN. 11 min., 1973, color*, 19

AFTERNOON OF A FAUN. 10 min., 1952 X, 19

AGNES DE MILLE'S A CHERRY TREE CAROL. 9 min., color, 1975, 19

AIR FOR THE G STRING. 7 min., 1934, b/w**, 20

ALICIA. 69 min., 1976, color, cinemascope*, 20

ALVIN AILEY—MEMORIES AND VISIONS. 54 min., color, 1975**, 20

AMERICAN BALLET COMPANY—ELIOT FELD, ARTISTIC DIRECTOR. 58 min., 1971, color*, 21

AMERICAN BALLET THEATRE: A CLOSE-UP IN TIME. 90 min., 1973, color**, 21

ANATOMY LESSON. 25min., 1968, color**, 22

ANN, A PORTRAIT. 24 min., 1973, color, 23

ANNA SOKOLOW DIRECTS—ODES. 40 min., 1972, b/w*, 23

APPALACHIAN SPRING. 31 min., 1958, b/w**, 23

ART AND TECHNIQUE OF THE BALLET. 11 min., 23

ART IS. 28 min., color, 23

ASSEMBLAGE. 59 min., 1968, color, 23

ATTIC SONGS. 15 min., color, 1975, 23

ATTITUDES IN DANCE. 28 min., 1964, b/w**, 23

BAGGAGE. 22 min., b/w, 1969, 23

BALANCHINE BALLET FILMS (CANADA)?, 24

BALANCHINE BALLET FILMS (GERMANY)?, 24

BALLERINA. 81 min., 1950, b/w*, 24

BALLERINA. 94 min., 1966, color, 24

BALLET ADAGIO. 10 min., 1971, color**, 25

BALLET BY DEGAS. 6 min., 1951, color, 25

BALLET CONCERT. 55 min., 1951, b/w*, 25

BALLET FOR ALL: SEVEN BALLET HISTORY FILMS*, 25

BALLET FOR ALL—1: HOW BALLET BEGAN. 26 min., 1970, b/w, 26

BALLET FOR ALL—2: BALLET ENTERS THE WORLD STAGE. 28 min., 1970, b/w*, 26

BALLET FOR ALL—3: HOW BALLET WAS SAVED. 29 min., 1970, b/w*, 26

BALLET FOR ALL—4: TCHAIKOVSKY AND THE RUSSIANS. 27 min., 1970, b/w*, 26

BALLET FOR ALL—5: THE BEGINNINGS OF TODAY. 27 min., 1970, b/w*, 27

BALLET FOR ALL—6: BALLET COMES TO BRITAIN. 26 min., 1970, b/w*, 27

BALLET FOR ALL—7: BRITISH BALLET TODAY. 29 min., 1970, b/w**, 27

BALLET GIRL. 23 min., b/w, 27

BALLET IN JAZZ. 11 min., 27

BALLET OF THE PARIS OPERA. 9 min., 1930s, b/w, 27

BALLET OF THE 20TH CENTURY—AMERICAN DEBUT. 20 min., color*, 28

BALLET WITH EDWARD VILLELLA. 27 min., 1970, color*, 28

BALLET'S GOLDEN AGE. 10 min., 1957, color, 28

BASHFUL BALLERINA. 19 min., 1937, b/w, 28

BAYADERKA. 10 min., 1943, b/w*, 28

BEAUTY AND THE BEAST BALLET. 50 min., color, 28

BEAUTY KNOWS NO PAIN. 25 min., 1973, color*, 28

BEHIND THE SCENES WITH THE ROYAL BALLET. 30 min., 1965, b/w*, 28

BEJART. 18 min., 1961, b/w, 28

BEJART FILMS, 29

THE BIX PIECES. 30 min., 1973, color, videotape**, 29

BLACK TIGHTS. 120 min., 1962, color, 29

BLUE STUDIO. 10 min., 1977, color, videotape*, 29

THE BODY AS AN INSTRUMENT, 29

BOLERO. 15 min., 1960s, b/w*, 29

THE BOLSHOI BALLET. 99 min., 1956, color?**, 29

THE BOLSHOI BALLET TOURS AMERICA. 45 min., 1959, b/w?, 29

BRANDENBURG CONCERTO NO. 4. 11 min., 1963, b/w, 30

CAMERA THREE. A series of 30 min. videotapes**, 30

CANADA AT 8:30. 28 min., color, 30

CAPRICCIO ESPAGNOL, see SPANISH FIESTA

CARNIVAL OF RHYTHM. 20 min., 1941, color, 30

CAROUSEL. 128 min., 1956, color*, 30

CHERRY TREE CAROL, 30

CHILDREN OF THEATRE STREET. 90 min., 1977, color, 30

A CHOREOGRAPHER AT WORK. 29 min., 1960, b/w, 30

CHOREOGRAPHY. 11 min., 1960, b/w, 30

CHRONIQUES DE FRANCE. A series of 25 min., b/w films, 31

CHRYSALLIS. 22 min., 1973, color*, 31

CINDERELLA. 80 min., 1961, color, 31

CIRCLES II. 8 min., 1974, color*, 31

CLAIRE DE LUNE. 5 min., color, 31

CLASSICAL BALLET. 29 min., 1960, b/w*, 31

COLLEGE KALEIDESCOPE. 29 min., color, 31

CONCERT OF STARS. 86 min., 1952, b/w, 31

CONTEMPORARY DANCE SERIES. 1970, b/w?, 31

CONTINUUM. 20 min., 1965, b/w, 31

CONVERSATION IN THE ARTS: DANCE. 21 min., color, 31

COPPELIA. 8 min., b/w X, 31

CORTEGE OF EAGLES. 38 min., 1969, color**, 31

CUBA—ART AND REVOLUTION. 46 min., 1971, color, 32

THE DANCE. 74 min., b/w, 32

DANCE: ANNA SOKOLOW'S ROOMS. 30 min., 1966, b/w**, 32

DANCE—A REFLECTION OF OUR TIMES. 29 min., 1960, b/w*, 32

DANCE AS AN ART FORM*, 32

DANCE CHROMATIC. 7 min., 1959, color, 33

DANCE CLASS. 9 min., color, 33

DANCE: ECHOES OF JAZZ. 29 min., 1965, b/w*, 33

DANCE FESTIVAL. 11 min., 1938, b/w, 33

DANCE: FOUR PIONEERS. 29 min., 1965, b/w**, 33

DANCE IN AMERICA**, 34

DANCE IN DARK AND LIGHT. 8 min., 1970, color?, 34

DANCE: IN SEARCH OF "LOVERS." 29 min., 1966, b/w*, 34

DANCE INSTRUMENT. Five films, each 16-19 min., 1975, b/w, 34

DANCE IN THE SUN. 7 min., 1953, b/w?, 34

DANCE: NEW YORK CITY BALLET. 29 min., 1965, b/w**, 34

DANCE OF ECSTASY. 12 min., color, widescreen, 34

THE DANCE ON FILM: 1894-1912, PART I, BALLET. 20 min., color*, 35

THE DANCE ON FILM: 1894-1912, PART II, THE ART DANCER. 15 min., b/w*, 35

DANCE: ROBERT JOFFREY BALLET. 30 min., 1965, b/w**, 35

DANCE THEATRE OF ALWIN NIKOLAIS. 31 min., 1964, b/w X, 35

DANCERS IN SCHOOL. 28 min., 1972, color, 35

A DANCER'S GRAMMAR. 16 min., 1977, color*, 35

A DANCER'S WORLD. 30 min., 1957, b/w**, 35

DANCES BY SUZUSHI HANAYAGI. 18 min., 1963, color, 36

THE DANCING PROPHET. 27 min., 1970, color, 36

DAY ON EARTH. 21 min., 1978, color**, 36

DENISHAWN. 10 min., b/w, 36

THE DESPERATE HEART. 9 min., late 1940s, b/w*, 36

DR. COPPELIUS. 97 min., 1968, color, 36

DON QUIXOTE. 109 min., 1973, color**, 36

DORIS CHASE. Six films, 4-8 min. each, color, 37

DREAM BALLERINA, see BALLERINA, 1950

DREAM OF AN ALCHEMIST. 12 min., color?, 37

DROTTNINGHOLM COURT THEATRE. 28 min., 1966, color, 37

THE SHAKERS.  15 min., 1940, b/w, silent*, 60

THE SHAKERS.  9 min., 1967, b/w, 60

SHAPE, 60

SHE AND MOON DANCES.  14 min., 1940s, silent?, 60

SLEEPING BEAUTY.  92 min., 1964, color, cinemascope**, 60

SOVIET ARMY SONG AND DANCE ENSEMBLE, 61

SPACE, 61

SPANISH FIESTA (CAPRICCIO ESPAGNOL).  20 min., 1941, color, 61

SPIRIT OF THE DANCE (LE SPECTRE DE LA DANSE).  22 min., 1965, b/w*, 61

SPRING NIGHT.  10 min., 1935, b/w*, 61

SQUAREGAME.  27 min., 1978, b/w, videotape, 61

STARS OF THE RUSSIAN BALLET.  80 min., 1953, b/w*, 61

STARS OF THE RUSSIAN BALLET—SWAN LAKE.  33 min., 1953, b/w, 62

STEPS OF THE BALLET.  25 min., 1948, b/w, 62

STORY.  20 min., 1964, b/w, 62

STRAVINSKY.  52 min., 1966, b/w*, 62

STUDY IN CHOREOGRAPHY FOR CAMERA.  4 min., 1940s, b/w, silent, 62

SUE'S LEG:  REMEMBERING THE THIRTIES.  59 min., 1976, color**, 62

SUGAR PLUM FAIRY VARIATION FROM THE BALLET "THE NUTCRACKER."  3 min., 1941, b/w, 63

SURE, I CAN DANCE.  25 min., color, 63

SWAN LAKE.  10 min., 1930s, b/w, 63

SWAN LAKE.  23 min., 1949, b/w, 63

SWAN LAKE.  81 min., 1959, color?, 63

SWAN LAKE, 63

SWEDEN:  FIRE AND ICE.  52 min., 1964, b/w**, 63

LES SYLPHIDES.  4 min., 1952, b/w, 63

TALES OF HOFFMANN.  118 min., 1951, color*, 63

TALES OF THE VIENNA WOODS.  9 min., 1949, b/w, 64

TARANTOS.  81 min., 1963, color, 64

THIS IS "THE PLACE."  35 min., color, 64

THREE BY GRAHAM.  1969, color**, 64

THREE DANCES 1964.  17 min., 1964, b/w, 64

THREE EPITAPHS.  6 min., 1966, b/w X*, 64

TIME, 64

A TIME TO DANCE.  29 min., 1960, b/w*, 64

TONIGHT WE SING.  109 min., 1953, color, 64

TOTEM.  16 min., color, 1963*, 64

TOUR EN L'AIR.  50 min., color, 1974**, 65

TRIADISCHE BALLETT (TRIADIC BALLET).  32 min., late 1960s, color**, 65

TRICK DANCE FILM.  11 min., 1926, b/w, silent, 65

TRIKFILM NO. 1.  1 min., color X, 65

USA:  DANCE**, 65

VARIATIONS AND CONCLUSION OF NEW DANCE—RECORD FILM.  7 min., 1978, color*, 65

VARIATIONS V.  1965, 50 min., b/w?*, 65

THE VERY EYE OF NIGHT.  14 min., 1958, b/w, 65

A VIDEO EVENT, PART 1 and PART 2.  30 min. each, 1974, color, videotape**, 65

VIDEO EXCHANGE, ?, 66

WALKAROUND TIME.  48 min., 1973, color**, 66

WASH.  11 min., 1971, color, 67

WATCHING BALLET.  35 min., 1965, b/w, 67

WESTBETH.  33 min., 1975, b/w*, 67

WINNING.  30 min., 1975, color, videotape*, 67

WITH MY RED FIRES.  31 min., 1978, color**, 67

WITH MY RED FIRES—RECORD FILM.  31 min., 1978, color*, 68

WORLD'S YOUNG BALLET.  70 min., 1969, b/w*, 68

YOUNG MAN AND DEATH (JEUNE HOMME ET LA MORT).  15 min., 1965, color**, 69